HOW TO INCREASE YOUR FAITH AND LIVE
A BOLD AND ABUNDANT LIFE IN CHRIST

BOLD & CRAZY Faith

The Inspirational

Daryn Carl Ramsey

Trina,
Thank you so much for your support! I pray that God continues to bless you. Remember to
[signature]

Copyright © 2019 by Daryn Carl Ramsey
All rights reserved.

Printed in the United States of America
ISBN 978-1-7335607-0-2

Requests for information should be addressed to:

darynramsey@diamondandlight.com

Published by Diamond & Light Publishing, LLC,
Belcamp, MD 21017

Unless otherwise stated, all Scripture citations are from King James Version. Public Domain; THE HOLY BIBLE, NEW INTERNATIONL VERSION®, NIV® Copyright © 1973, 1978, 1984, 2011 by Biblica, Inc. ™ Used by permission. All rights reserved worldwide. Scripture quotations from New King James Version (NKJV), copyright © 1979, 1980, 1982, Thomas Nelson Publishers, Inc. Scripture quotations from THE MESSAGE. Copyright © by Eugene H. Peterson 1993, 1994, 1995, 1996, 2000, 2001, 2002. Used by permission of Tyndale House Publishers, Inc. Scripture quotations from The Holy Bible, English Standard Version® (ESV®) Copyright © 2001 by Crossway, a publishing ministry of Good News Publishers. All rights reserved. Used by permission.

All rights reserved. No part of this publication may be reproduced, stored electronically or otherwise, transmitted in any form or by any means, including but not limited to electronic, mechanical, photocopying or recording—except brief quotations and printed reviews—without permission of the publisher.

Edited by The Comprehensive Editing, Writing & Publishing Company, LLC, Raleigh, NC 27609

CONTENTS

ENDORSEMENTS

Daryn Ramsey lays out for his readers the clear and true message of faith and how it empowers and encourages every believer. He has taken his excitement for Christ and penned a work that lays out the foundational truths every believer needs.

- Bishop Walter Scott Thomas Sr., Pastor, New Psalmist Baptist Church Baltimore, MD., Presiding Prelate Kingdom Association of Covenant Pastors, and Certified Executive Coach

Daryn Carl Ramsey is remarkably brilliant as he presents a stimulating unique prospective and creative approach to inspire believers to increase their **fearless faith.** He uses both biblical and contemporary faith building principles and techniques to deliver his message of acquiring *BOLD & CRAZY FAITH* to truly live the blessed and abundant life, even when the world is being affected by the devastating impact of social and economic woes and epidemics. He captures the Christian journey, Christian lifestyle and faith building all together.

-Dr. Missy Johnson, International Best-Selling Author, 2017 President Barack Obama Lifetime Achievement Award Recipient, 2018 Michigan Chronicle Women of Excellence Award Recipient, Reinvention Strategist, BreakFree Coach and Life Architect to Women

DEDICATION

I dedicate *Bold & Crazy Faith* to my wonderful, beautiful, and loving wife Deborah, who has been there with me, for me, and by my side every step of the way. Deb, I honor, cherish, and love you dearly!

I also dedicate this book to our daughter Monet, grandson Jalen and the entire family.

A special dedication to my loving parents, the late Carl and Arlene Ramsey, who loved, cared, taught and provided for me. They both sacrificed, worked very hard and did an awesome job raising me. Without their patience and influence, I would not be the person that I am today.

ACKNOWLEDGEMENTS

Thank you to my two brothers Gary and Brian and my sister Cheryl. Each of you has made a positive impact on my life and have helped me to be the man that I am today. I love and appreciate you all!

Special thank you and shout out to my pastor Bishop Walter Scott Thomas Sr., Diaconate and the entire leadership and congregation of the New Psalmist Baptist Church who have helped me to grow as a person and servant leader to fulfill the will of God in my life.

I especially want to thank my mentor Tressa Azarel who I knew from the outset was a godsend for me. Tressa is a gifted and multi-talented publisher and executive producer in the movie industry who has blessed me significantly with her expertise in writing and publishing, overall business acumen and spirit. I also want to thank the amazing Pam Perry who is a PR giant and branding accelerator icon for being my public relations and media mentor.

Finally. a very special thank you to God who heard and answered my cry many years ago and assured me on one special day with these words, "Everything is going to be all right! From that day forward, my life has never been the same. Thank you, Lord!!! I dedicate this book to You, and You already know that I have dedicated my life to You.

INTRODUCTION

I wrote this book to help Christian believers significantly increase their faith so that they can live more productive lives. In the Christian journey, growth and development take place over time primarily through the inspiration and confidence that come with believing, reading, and applying God's word. *Bold & Crazy Faith* is knowing that you will live a victorious life, because of your relationship as a child of God, and your personal intimate connection with Jesus Christ. *Bold & Crazy Faith* will meet all believers where they are in their Christian journey.

This book is an excellent resource for new followers of Christ who are beginning to build their faith, or for believers who, for some time, have wanted to gain confidence through the word. *Bold & Crazy Faith* will stimulate you and provoke a burning desire to   secure the level of faith that you need to live the abundant life that Jesus promised.

After reading this book, you will be prepared to live boldly through the exhilaration of joy and the agony of pain. You will learn how to sustain your faith through heartache and pain, and even have *Bold & Crazy Faith* during those times you will have to go toe-to-toe with Satan.

Bold & Crazy Faith will motivate you to be bold even when God is silent and navigate you around negative influences and associations that would otherwise hold you down. Further, this book will equip you with the knowledge that you need to not only prevent defeat, but to also persevere boldly through difficult times, which we all face. Here's the bottom line about facing any consequence: it takes *Bold & Crazy Faith* to motivate you to lean on God's promises, which are His assurance to living the abundant life in the face of difficult times.

By faith, you will be inspired through real-life experiences I have had as well as experiences and persecution that other believers have encountered in their journey. Lastly, *Bold & Crazy Faith* leverages profound quotes and wisdom from world renown authorities on the word of God.

CHAPTER 1

Building Your Faith

> *"Not only is your story your truth, your story is going to be the platform and the foundation for everything that's getting ready to happen in your life."*

— **DeVon Franklin**

INSPIRATION

A s a believer, you need to have *Bold & Crazy Faith*! The bolder and crazier your faith, the greater your Father will reward you. The bible says, "And without faith it is impossible to please God, because anyone who comes to him must believe that he exists and that he rewards those who earnestly seek him" (Hebew11:6). There is no limit to what God can do in your life. Therefore glory to him who is able to do immeasurably more than all we can ask or imagine, according to His power that is at work in us (Ephesians 3:20 NIV).

God wants us to have *Bold & Crazy Faith*. But if we were honest, most of us may not have the kind of faith that can move mountains. Building your faith takes time. So, to have that *Bold & Crazy Faith* that God wants you to have, let's dig in and start from the beginning. Your beginning may be right now as a new babe in Christ. You may even be afraid to share the good news with your family, friends and co-workers about your relationship with God because you are fearful that they may begin to act differently towards you. Or, maybe you are a Christian who has been walking with the Lord for some time but lack the confidence to boldly proclaim your faith. If this describes your Christian experience, just know, "For God has not given us a spirit of fear, but of power and of love and of a sound mind (2 Timothy 1:7 NIV).

LIFE EXPERIENCE

Let's look at the conversion experience to following Christ as a way to examine how your faith builds over time. When you were converted, you were born again in Christ. You made the decision to repent and turn from sin and to Christ. On that day, you decided to surrender your old life as you knew it and believe in your heart that the Lord Jesus Christ was the resurrected Son of God. There was a newness that took place. Thank God for salvation! The bible says, "For it is by grace you have been saved, through faith-and this is not from yourselves, it is the gift of God-not by works, so that no one can boast" (Ephesians 2:8,9, NIV). You had faith already back then. The bible also says in Romans 12:3 "that God hath dealt to every man the measure of faith." Hey, come on now, so if you now know this, there is absolutely no way in the world you should not have *Bold & Crazy Faith!* When you received salvation, something amazing happened to you. You felt a bit lighter on your feet. There was some pep in your step. You became a new creature as well as a son or daughter of God, and it felt good. Right! Look how the bible states your conversion in Romans 8:12-17 (NIV).

"Therefore, brothers and sisters, we have an obligation-but it is not to the flesh, to live according to it. For if you live according to the flesh, you will die; but if by the Spirit you put to death the mis

deeds of the body, you will live. For those who are led by the Spirit of God are the children of God. [15] The Spirit you received does not make you slaves, so that you live in fear again; rather, the Spirit you received brought about your adoption to sonship.[a] And by him we cry, "Abba,[b] Father." [16] The Spirit himself testifies with our spirit that we are God's children. [17] Now if we are children, then we are heirs—heirs of God and co-heirs with Christ, if indeed we share in his sufferings in order that we may also share in his glory".

Soon thereafter you learned to read your bible and discovered that the Gospel is the good news of Christ. The bible says, "Like newborn babies, crave pure spiritual milk, so that by it you may grow up in your salvation (1 Peter 2:2, NIV). As a new believer this was an exciting time! The Christian life had become a new lifestyle to you. You attended church more often or on a regular basis. For those readers that got saved a long time ago, my question to you is this: do you remember when you were on fire for the Lord? I sincerely believe that it was during that time early in your walk with Christ that you began to experience the truth about this journey.

You begin to see firsthand that when you draw nearer to God, He will draw nearer to you. You begin to experience blessing after blessing. The "wow" moments in your life are coming in like rapid fire. This is when you say to yourself, 'What have I been doing all these years? I was doing a little bit of this and a little bit of that, and all the time I never really believed that *Christianity* is what's up'. God is letting you know right up front. '*Get ready for the ride, my son, my daughter, you haven't seen anything yet. This is just the beginning*'. The Lord knows that currently as a new believer you are impressionable and vulnerable. You have decided to step out on faith to try new things, and He knows that he has your attention and wants to keep it. He wants you to stay the course, so he reveals himself to you often to let you know that he really is

13

there just as he said in his word. If he didn't reveal himself often, then you may not have been able to sustain and not return to things that would have kept you stagnant and stale. It is during this time and these experiences that you begin building your faith.

Conversely, God knows that early on, people will notice the change in you. Some even try to remind you of your past. They will remind you of things that have transpired in the not so distant past that you may not be proud of. Just know that this is the work of the devil whose mission is to steal, kill and destroy. The devil is a liar. He will work through people and situations to distract you from making a positive impact in the lives of others. Satan wants to steal your faith and boldness to stand for Christ. Don't fret, no weapon will prosper. Greater is he that is in you, than he that is in the world (1 John 4:4, KJV). Jesus explained to the disciples that he is never alone as the father was always with him. In like manner, Jesus is with you all the time. Jesus goes on to say, "I have told you these things, so that in me you may have peace. In this world you will have trouble. But take heart! I have overcome the world." (John 16:33, NIV). We have the victory through him.

The devil would like to take the word of God from your mouth, your ears and your life. If you want to be the best that you can be, you will have to limit and sever associations with some people. I cannot stress this enough. This is absolutely necessary. Take inventory of your circles and determine who has your best interest because some people can lead you back to places that you no longer want to be. Some former associations may also influence you to do things that you no longer want to do. Never underestimate how quickly you can lose everything that you have worked hard for in your Christian journey because of one bad decision that was influenced by someone else. It is vital to examine, therefore, the motives of people that are trying to persuade you to do things. While there are no perfect people or perfect circles, you still need to be very selective when it comes to associations. Be careful of some people that want to be around you. It only takes one bad decision that will have you backsliding so hard and fast that it will be very difficult to get back the faith that you had built up. It is very hard to get off the ropes when you are fighting for your life.

BIBLICAL EXAMPLE

Noah had the kind of faith that was not only bold but also brave and daring. In his generation, wickedness among mankind was normal and was considered customary. However, Noah trusted God and exercised faith in executing God's command to build an Ark.

BOLD CONCLUSION

Please understand this in its context. Remember that you are not perfect. No one is. Making a mistake is not a reason to throw in the towel. At the same time, however, God does not like you to be lukewarm, which means that you are not fully committed to him. Some Christians only abide and obey out of convenience. When things are going well in their lives, they are Gods biggest cheerleaders. But when the trials and storms come, they are no longer proclaiming the name of Jesus. Trials and storms test your faith. God is still good even in bad times. No riding the fence. He wants you to be unapologetic about your new life and the good news of Jesus Christ. Jesus says, "Whoever is not with me is against me, and whoever does not gather with me scatters" (Luke 11:23, NIV). You are a part of the greatest family that ever existed! You are joint heirs with Christ! That's right! It does not get any better than this. Activate your faith and take a stand with crazy boldness today for your Lord and Savior Jesus Christ! He is counting on you.

CHAPTER 1-BUILDING YOUR FAITH
BOLD OBSERVATIONS

_____

_____

_____

_____

_____

_____

_____

_____

_____

_____

_____

_____

_____

_____

_____

CHAPTER 1-BUILDING YOUR FAITH
BOLD OBSERVATIONS

_____

_____

_____

_____

_____

_____

_____

_____

_____

_____

_____

_____

_____

_____

_____

_____

CHAPTER 1-BUILDING YOUR FAITH
BOLD OBSERVATIONS

_____

_____

_____

_____

_____

_____

_____

_____

_____

_____

_____

_____

_____

_____

CHAPTER 1-BUILDING YOUR FAITH
BOLD OBSERVATIONS

_____

_____

_____

_____

_____

_____

_____

_____

_____

_____

_____

_____

_____

_____

_____

_____

CHAPTER 1-BUILDING YOUR FAITH
BOLD OBSERVATIONS

_____

_____

_____

_____

_____

_____

_____

_____

_____

_____

_____

_____

_____

_____

_____

_____

CHAPTER 1-BUILDING YOUR FAITH
FINAL OBSERVATIONS & ACTIONS

CHAPTER 2

Self Confidence through the Word

*"God has invested entirely too much in you for you to be
comfortable in anything less than you were created to be."*

— **T.D. Jakes**

INSPIRATION

A s you grow in Christ, you gain self-confidence through
hearing and reading God's word. Consequently, faith
comes from hearing the message, and the message is heard
through the word about Christ (Romans 10:17, NIV). The more you
hear the word, the more your faith increases. When you study your
bible or write notes from a sermon, your faith increases steadily because the word of God is living and breathing. In 2 Timothy 3:16
(ESV), the bible says, " All Scripture is breathed out by God and
profitable for teaching, for reproof, for correction, and for training
in righteousness."

Therefore memorizing Scripture is important to help you
remember what God has said. Scripture memorization can also be
used in prayer when and where applicable. As such, consuming the
word of God regularly and consistently is key in developing a self-
confidence that eventually transforms into bold faith.

Even more, the word is inspired by God. The word is captivating and interesting. The word is written to motivate you. The word of God is intended to encourage you and comfort you. The word of God is intended to give you direction. The word of God is intended to give you instruction. The word of God is intended to give you guidance. The word of God exists to give you knowledge about yourself and about God. It provides wisdom so that you can make informed decisions and steer clear from danger.

LIFE EXPERIENCE

Today, in the 21st Century, the word has become widespread. For instance, thanks to technology many of us have unlimited access to get the word of God anytime you want it. The word is shared through more traditional means such as television and radio, Christian movies, plays, and magazines all of which have grown steadily with the word of God. Currently, computers, tablets, smartphones, and smart television sets have opened the door to a social media explosion where APPS and platforms like YouTube, Facebook, Twitter, Instagram, Snapchat, and Podcast have made the word accessible at the touch of a screen. Technology has come a long way.

You can get the word from listening to Christian music as well. It is a known fact that people have preferences when it comes to learning and enjoyment. For instance, some people prefer to learn audibly versus visually, meaning they become more efficient at learning by listening than learning by seeing material. Similarly, some people prefer Christian rap music verses praise and worship. Let's take it a step further. Some people are not avid readers, and some cannot read at all. From that vantage point, Christian music provides yet another alternative to learn the word of God as the lyrics are inspired by God, Scripture and others' Christian life experiences. There are many genres of Christian music to include Contemporary

Christian, Christian Pop, Traditional Gospel, Southern Gospel, Gospel Jazz, Gospel Reggae, and the list goes on. As you can see there are many ways to ingest the word of God daily. Take notice in the way I used the word "ingest". I did this intentionally to make a serious point. You should take in the word of God daily in much the same way that you do "food". The word is just as valuable. We need food to live and survive just as we need the word of God to live and survive.

In sum, the word is living and inspired by God to give you guidance and direction in your life. In much the same way that your attendance and participation in church is critical to building your faith, staying in the word is critical to the self-confidence you will gain through the word. I have seen many people that attended worship service on a regular basis become spotty in their attendance and soon thereafter stop going. That is why taking in the word regularly in various forms is the key to becoming self-confident through the word.

BIBLICAL EXAMPLE

The Holy Bible is the best-selling book of all-time, and why wouldn't it be? If you are looking to find the answers to life, I encourage you to look to God's word. Abraham had bold and crazy faith. If he didn't, he wouldn't have gathered his family and things together to leave home and travel to an unfamiliar location in obedience to God. He trusted God and made his home, living in tents as he traveled from place to place until God confirmed his destination. And so extraordinary was Abraham's faith in God that he was willing to sacrifice his beloved son upon God's word. "By faith, Abraham, when God tested him, offered Isaac as a sacrifice" (Hebrews 11:17 NIV).

BOLD CONCLUSION

When trouble has you down, I implore you to read God's word. If you need encouragement, listen to God's word. When you are looking for the right things to say, pick up the word. God's word is considered the sword of the spirit and can be used to stand firm against the schemes of the enemy. The bible declares that the word is sharper than any two-edged sword. Today, not even Google can compare to that.

As you grow your self-confidence through the word, you will recognize the power that you have within. No, not at the beginning of your Christian journey, but eventually over time, you will have a boldness that breaks through ceilings and knocks down doors. As a reward, God can position you to become a trailblazer in your career or family allowing you to break through ceilings that had never been broken before.

You will come to realize the Holy Spirit gives you knowledge of things that you had not even realized before. With that said, you will become bold! The bible says, "But you will receive power, when the Holy Spirit comes on you (Acts1:8 NIV)." As such, you will be set apart gradually and steadily through the truth of the word to use your gifts for God's purposes.

Admittedly, He is the way the truth and the life, but that's not it. God's word never changes. When you are hurting the word will encourage you. It is at those times when using the word boldly in prayer reinforces your self-confidence.

Take God at his word, for His word shall not return unto him void. When you use God's word in prayer, you are letting Him know that you trust Him to do what he said He will do. It gives you bold confidence because your prayers are reinforced and influenced by the word of God and is the foundation of your prayer. In turn, the person that is the recipient of the prayer gains confidence in knowing the word for themselves or will have confidence that you know the word and know how to apply it in prayer.

Understand that God rewards your obedience and your trust in Him. Therefore, when God tells you in His word to study, trust that you will find. When God says, knock and the door will be open to you, trust that He will reward you for seeking Him and open doors that you never imagined. God rewards your diligence when you turn to him for guidance. The bible declares, "He rewards those who earnestly seek Him (Hebrews 11:6, NIV).

So, as you grow and see the results of God's faithfulness and truth, your faith continues to increase. You begin to trust God and become much bolder in your faith. Celebrate your new Christian lifestyle, self-confidence and victories. Be proud and unapologetic about your new-found boldness. Do not be ashamed of the Gospel of Jesus Christ and be inspired by the word. The word of God is your inspiration.

CHAPTER 2-SELF CONFIDENCE THROUGH THE WORLD

BOLD OBSERVATIONS

_____

_____

_____

_____

_____

_____

_____

_____

_____

_____

_____

_____

_____

_____

_____

CHAPTER 2-SELF CONFIDENCE THROUGH THE WORLD
FINAL OBSERVATIONS & ACTIONS

_____

_____

_____

_____

_____

_____

_____

_____

_____

_____

_____

_____

_____

_____

_____

_____

CHAPTER 3

Dreaming Big Visualize Your Future

"Keep your dreams alive. Understand to achieve anything requires faith and belief in yourself, vision, hard work, determination, and dedication. Remember all things are possible for those who believe."

— **Gail Devers**

INSPIRATION

Did you know that it takes a tremendous amount of faith to dream big and believe that you are going to accomplish what you set out to? It takes even more confidence to visualize and see yourself in your future. As the Word of God states, "Now faith is confidence in what we hope for and assurance about what we do not see" (Hebrews 11:1, NIV). A person who has *Bold & Crazy Faith* is dreaming big on a regular basis. Not only are they dreaming big, but also, they are regularly making things happen. The important thing to note here is that they are not making things happen on their own. They know that their help comes from the Lord. They routinely activate their faith to become highly productive in their endeavors. They know how and intentionally activate

35

the power that lives within. The power that lives within is none other than the Holy Spirit who revives you and brings a newness that enhances your life.

I'm sure that you have heard the saying, "Actions speak louder than words." This holds true even in a spirit-filled life. For example, your regular worship has not gone unnoticed. God sees the reverence that you are giving Him and the praises for what He has done in your life. Your service inside and outside the church reflects the dedication that you have to God and people. God sees what you are doing. He has blessings prepared to release to you accordingly. God sees the strides, growth and obedience that you have made in your giving. The Lord loves a cheerful giver and really will pour out blessings that you don't have room to receive. It is because of these things you can dream big. For these reasons you can visualize and see your future.

In simple terms, God's word says what he will do, and God does what His word says. Dreaming big requires being inspired by the word of God. The word teaches us that we serve a big God who is limitless. He is all-powerful and all-knowing. You will have big dreams when you truly believe that you can do all things through Christ who strengthens you.

God has given you everything that you need to fulfill your vision and your dream, if the dream lines up with the purposes that He has for your life. My pastor, says that we all need to ask ourselves this question: Does this line up with the will of God concerning me? So, when you are dreaming big and visualizing yourself in your future, ask the question, *Is the dream lining up with the will of God concerning me?*

To fulfill the vision that God has given you takes more than courage. In fact, it takes great faith to make these dreams come to fruition. So, execute the *Bold & Crazy Faith* that you have in your-self and your Lord and Savior Jesus Christ. Stir up the gift that re-sides deep down in your soul. Draw from your knowledge of scripture, wisdom and experience. Administer the power that works in you to achieve, accomplish and prosper in your dreams.

When God has given you a vision, take full advantage of the opportunity. If God is in it, you always win. The enemy is al-ready defeated, and the battle is already won. It's like the game mo-nopoly and the get out of jail card or a free prize behind door number one on the gameshow *The Price is Right*. It's always a win-win situation. If God is for us, who can be against us (Romans 8:31, NIV). God will always provide the tools and resources as well as the instructions to get you on the path to making your dreams be-come a reality. We just must listen keenly as he goes about his busi-ness in doing so. Listening keenly may not come solely in the sense of hearing him speak audibly. Listening keenly may be recognizing when he has placed a person in your life to guide you to the next step in the process. It may be realizing a door that has been shut was the work of God redirecting you into the right path that was designed to take you to your dream and destiny that he has accord-ing to his purposes that he has for you. "I will instruct you and teach you in the way you should go; I will counsel you with my loving eye on you" (Psalm 32:8, NIV).

LIFE EXPERIENCE

I remember when I began to dream big many years ago. The day that I surrendered my heart and gave my life to Christ was a day that I will always remember. It was on this day that my life changed forever. I was a mess and was having a rough time with life. The Lord said to me, "Everything is going to be all right". He assured me through the Spirit, "Everything was going to be all right". I almost couldn't believe it at that time in my life. It was the most amazing thing that ever happened to me. Literally! Right then and there. I knew without a shadow of a doubt that all my worries and pain were over. I absolutely knew that the storm was over! It was over. I had a new beginning, a new life. Right away I began to think about all my new possibilities. I now had a new belief that so many of the things that I once thought was impossible were now possible. They would just take some work, but they were fully possible because the Lord told me that everything was going to be all right. Right away I knew that God intended for me to be in a field that was directly correlated to helping people. It wasn't one of those thoughts or decisions that I made because I thought that it would be the right thing to do. No, I knew that I needed to be doing something that helped people. I went to the library to research careers that helped people. Some of the careers that I searched were in counseling, social work, case worker, education, nurse and even medicine. The field that drew most of my attention was social work. To gain insight into this career, I talked to a few ministers who were also social workers. Lord would have it that I would eventually become a servant leader as an ordained Deacon and a civil servant with the Department of Defense. I was in the right ballpark from the start. And we know that in all things God works for the good of those who love him, who have been called according to His purpose (Romans 8:28 NIV).

As my Lord continued to provide, I received overflow in so many areas of my life. My wife who I love with all my heart has been a tremendous blessing in my life and a support system in my quest to complete this book. He who finds a wife finds what is good and receives favor from the Lord (Proverbs 18:22 NIV).

This book for me is putting my money where my mouth is, *Bold & Crazy Faith*! This was a huge endeavor and a dream come true. Just in case you don't believe me, my faith is so bold that I am already working on my second book in which I will surprise you with the title and genre later.

BIBLICAL EXAMPLE

The bible teaches in the book of Genesis that Joseph was well associated with dreams. Not only could he understand his own dreams, he also had the gift to interpret the dreams of others. For example, while in jail from being falsely accused of sexual assault, Joseph interprets the dreams of two inmates that were formally Pharaoh's butler and baker. Joseph interprets accurately that the butler would be acquitted, and the baker would be put to death. It wasn't until Joseph correctly interprets Pharaoh's disturbing dreams that he was freed. Joseph's interpretation of seven years of abundance and seven years of famine allows Pharaoh to prepare Egypt for the famine and puts Joseph in his good grace. Pharaoh appointed Joseph as second in command to himself.

BOLD CONCLUSION

Just as Joseph dreamed and fulfilled the plan that God had for his life, you can do the same. To fulfill your dream, you need unshakable faith that endures. He didn't just throw you a couple of bones because he felt sorry for you and is now done with you. No, no, no! You are down with the baddest and greatest thing that this universe has ever encountered. And God is down with you, too. Forever. God has invested in you eternally. As you really begin to get it deep down in your soul that God is with you for the long haul, your mindset will transform to expect greater.

Just like Mase told the world and not only Diddy, "I thought I told you that we won't stop, I thought I told you that we won't stop". God is saying to you through his word, "I thought I told you that we won't stop." You see, God wants you to do your part, too. It's a team effort. He never wants you to stop working for Him, working for others and working for yourself. God will never stop working for you.

The bible declares everyone born of God overcomes the world. This is the victory that has overcome the world, even our faith. Who is it that overcomes the world? Only the one who believes that Jesus is the Son of God (1 John 5:4-5 NIV). There is absolutely no excuse or reasoning to feel any other way if you truly believe and have an intimate relationship with God. You can have no limits to what you can do when you have God in your life because the bible tells us that "a man's gift makes room for him, And brings him before great men (Proverbs 18:16, NIV).

The Lord reminds us through His word repeatedly that He is there for us. Even in the names that we have for God, Emanuel "God with us", Jehovah Jireh, "The Lord will provide. When we know this, how can we not have *Bold & Crazy Faith?*!

CHAPTER 3-DREAMING BIG VISUALIZE YOUR FUTURE
BOLD OBSERVATIONS

_____

_____

_____

_____

_____

_____

_____

_____

_____

_____

_____

_____

_____

_____

CHAPTER 3-DREAMING BIG VISUALIZE YOUR FUTURE

BOLD OBSERVATIONS

_____

_____

_____

_____

_____

_____

_____

_____

_____

_____

_____

_____

_____

_____

CHAPTER 3-DREAMING BIG VISUALIZE YOUR FUTURE
BOLD OBSERVATIONS

CHAPTER 3-DREAMING BIG VISUALIZE YOUR FUTURE
BOLD OBSERVATIONS

_____

_____

_____

_____

_____

_____

_____

_____

_____

_____

_____

_____

_____

_____

CHAPTER 3-DREAMING BIG VISUALIZE YOUR FUTURE

BOLD OBSERVATIONS

_____

_____

_____

_____

_____

_____

_____

_____

_____

_____

_____

_____

_____

_____

_____

_____

CHAPTER 3-DREAMING BIG VISUALIZE YOUR FUTURE
FINAL OBSERVATIONS & ACTIONS

_____

_____

_____

_____

_____

_____

_____

_____

_____

_____

_____

_____

_____

_____

_____

_____

CHAPTER 4

Trusting God and Knowing

"It doesn't matter if a million people tell you what you can't do, or if ten million people tell you no. If you get one yes from God, that's all you need."

— **Tyler Perry**

INSPIRATION

As you develop maturity in the faith as a Christian, your trust in God continues to increase steadily. You have seen God deliver on his word over and over again. You have seen your Jehovah-Jireh provide for you when your money was funny. You have seen God heal you, family, and friends from sickness and disease. He has opened doors for you that you know would have never opened had it not been for Him. God has even protected you from your enemies who wanted to harm you.

Don't get me wrong. Even the most mature Christians worry and doubt from time to time. When you worry and doubt you are not trusting God as being active and present in your life. In doing so, you are placing limitations on God as if He is a part-time

God. Rest assured that He is an on-time God. God keeps his hand in our hand and never gives up on us always staying the course. The bible says, "One who has unreliable friends soon comes to ruin, but there is a friend who sticks closer than a brother (Proverbs 18:24, NIV).

As a mature Christian, you can trust God for almost anything that your heart desires. The bible says, "being confident of this, that he who began a good work in you will carry it on to completion until the day of Christ Jesus (Philippians 1:6, NIV). In Isaiah 26:3,4 (ESV) the bible says, "You keep him in perfect peace whose mind is stayed on you, because he trusts in you. Trust in the Lord forever, for the Lord God is an everlasting rock".

LIFE EXPERIENCE

Many years ago, I got a job as a customer accounts representative at a well- known company. The company provided one of the best employment opportunities in the area. It had a great reputation for providing good benefits and if you worked there it was as well regarded and reputable as having a good government job. At the time, I was dating my future wife Deb. We were just a year into starting our new relationship. We were both happy about the great career opportunity that this company afforded until I got the bad news. I was terminated for unsuccessful performance, along with two other employees. This all happened just one or two days before my employee probationary period expired.

The termination was a huge blow. I was within one year of starting a serious relationship with Deb and everything in my life was going well, then BAM! Fired! *Fired?* Getting fired was a surprise to me. It was also surprising to the others that were let go as well. One lady broke into tears after receiving the news. The four

48

of us had gone through an intense training that was almost unbelievable. This training was one of the most difficult processes that I ever had to go through in my life.

The trainer that we had was like a drill sergeant. She badgered us about everything. I remembered at the time thinking, "is this really necessary for a Customer Account position?" I never could wrap my mind around how difficult the training was and really thought that it was overkill on the part of the trainer.

I always considered myself a pretty quick learner at most things. Even the things that I have never really been strong in, like math, I would get it eventually unless I gave up. In this case, I worked very hard and was diligent in working on the training at home as well as work. My career was on the line. At the time, I felt that all I really needed to do was make it out of the training. If I made it out of training, I would be good out on the floor with repetition and experience. Now that I look at things in retrospect, I believe God undoubtedly had other plans for my life.

As I intimated, getting terminated shook me for a minute. I was pretty early in my walk with Christ. I always had the confidence of knowing that God told me, "Everything is going to be all right," a few years prior. But Satan has a way of stealing (snatching) your joy and tempting you to doubt even the things that you know you know. *That's right*, I responded inwardly, *know you know*. But God! I kept hearing but God! I kept trusting God! Hallelujah! That leads me into letting you know to hold on to this Scripture for yourself.

No temptation has seized you except what is common to man, And God is faithful; he will not let you be tempted beyond what you can bear, but when you are tempted, he will also provide a way out so that you can stand up under it (1 Corinthians 10:13, NIV).

To be honest, I had already acquired significant faith, but it has grown substantially since then. This new-found faith allowed me the opportunity to see some of the most beautiful homes that money could buy. It was here that I began to dream of one day owning a dream home that my wife Deb and I could be proud of.

I began to trust God and know that he would not only provide but bless us with a nice home one day. And He did. We relocated from New Jersey to Maryland and were able to buy our dream home. God is so awesome that three and one-half years later, He blessed us with another dream home even nicer than the first one.

The icing on the cake with the real cherry on the top was that he even allowed us to keep the first dream home and use it as an   investment property. Deb and I always wanted to have at least one investment property and had nearly purchased one in Virginia in 2006. God knew what He was doing then as well. He shut the door to the investment property as quickly as He shut the door to us relocating to Virginia. Consequently, in three and one-half years, God had not blessed us with one but two dream homes. Yes, He is that good! We are truly living in overflow. Praise be to God!

I never would have learned to trust and know God as a Customer Account Representative the way that I did as an Outside Sales Representative. The job called for me to go into the homes of prospective buyers and existing customers to sell a service. This job was an absolute blessing in my life in which I really learned about the true everlasting power of God. I will touch on this more at a later time. Powerful! Again, this job was such a blessing to me as I had just recently started a relationship with Deb and had just gotten fired from a great job where I was hoping to make a career.

BIBLICAL EXAMPLE

Rahab was a prostitute who ran a small inn that was constructed into the exterior wall of the city of Jericho. Although she was not thought of as an upstanding member in the community or one who most people would connect with spirituality, Rahab trusted God and had strong faith.

Joshua, the general of the Israelite armies, had sent scouts to Jericho to investigate their barricades. Right after the scouts completed their snooping of the walls, gates and guards, they visited Rahab's Inn. During their visit, someone eavesdropped on their plans to get out of the city safely. Meanwhile, the king of Jericho got wind that there were scouts at the inn and sent some of his men to trap them.

The king and the people of the city of Jericho knew all about Joshua's defeat of the Amalekites and that God had favor on the children of Jacob because he had delivered them out of Egypt. Rahab had heard about all of this as well and was sure that she would be killed as the city was demolished by Israel's army.

Upon their arrival at the Inn, the king's men were told by Rahab that the men they were looking for left just before nightfall. Rahab was taking a big chance as she hid the scouts at the top of her house under some bundles of dried flax. As the scouts were left undiscovered, Rahab asked the men to return her favor when the Israel army invaded the city. To show their gratitude upon being let down through her window with a scarlet thread by Rahab, the scouts told Rahab to tie this cord of scarlet thread in the window with the promise that she and her household would be saved during the invasion that was coming. By faith she was obedient and tied the scarlet cord in the window. Later as the walls came tumbling down and the Israelites seized the city of Jericho, Joshua commanded that Rahab and her family be spared.

Rahab did the things that are necessary when you have *Bold & Crazy Faith*: she believed, which means that she trusted God and she acted. Knowing that God had his hands on the Israelites, she believed the spies and exercised her faith by hanging the scarlet cord out the window. When Joshua and the Israelite army marched around the city of Jericho and began shouting, the walls surrounding the city crumbled. However, Rahab's household and possessions were spared as the Israelite army recognized the scarlet cord hanging from the window. The men who were favored by God kept their word, and the house of Rahab the prostitute stood tall above the ruins.

At the end, the spies brought Rahab and her family who were also in the house to Joshua. He thanked her and presented her with fertile land as a reward.

BOLD CONCLUSION

Trust God today and express your belief in Him by moving swiftly with *Bold & Crazy Faith*. If you believe, be bold in your expectations of God. He will be honored that you really believe that you can do all things through Christ and are not putting limitations on his capabilities. The bible declares in Ephesians 3:20 (NIV), "Now to him who is able to do immeasurably more than all we ask or imagine, according to his power that is at work within us".

The best way to know what God wants is to go to him yourself. You can go to God in devotional time on a regular, scheduled basis or randomly. The key thing here is that you are going to Him. The bible says, "And without faith it is impossible to please God, because anyone who comes to him must believe that he exists and that he rewards those who earnestly seek him" (Hebrews 11:6, NIV).

When you hear from God, move out on it in faith and trust that He will not steer you wrong, because He won't. In Philippians 4:17, God declares, "And my God will meet all your needs according to the riches of his glory in Christ Jesus" (NIV). Remember that He is the ALMIGHTY GOD and you are His child. He will not lead you into a direction that is harmful or fatal. Now let me be clear here about something. God will give us things that we need that we don't ask for as well. Sometimes they are things that we didn't bargain for, but He knows that we need these things to help us now and in the future. Let's face it, sometimes it's not pretty. The bible says, "because the Lord disciplines the one he loves, and he chastens everyone he accepts as his son." (Hebrews 12:6, NIV). Think about the punishment that you received from your parents that was given to you for correction and for your own good. Your Heavenly Father does the same thing for you because He loves you unconditionally. He wants you to grow into the destiny that He has already provided for you, and He wants you to get there for His purposes. He also wants to bless you along the way, but you have to seek, knock, trust and also listen intently.

CHAPTER 4 - TRUSTING GOD & KNOWING
BOLD OBSERVATIONS

_____

_____

_____

_____

_____

_____

_____

_____

_____

_____

_____

_____

_____

_____

CHAPTER 4 -TRUSTING GOD & KNOWING
BOLD OBSERVATIONS

CHAPTER 4 -TRUSTING GOD & KNOWING
BOLD OBSERVATIONS

_____

_____

_____

_____

_____

_____

_____

_____

_____

_____

_____

_____

_____

_____

CHAPTER 4 -TRUSTING GOD & KNOWING
BOLD OBSERVATIONS

_____

_____

_____

_____

_____

_____

_____

_____

_____

_____

_____

_____

_____

_____

CHAPTER 4 -TRUSTING GOD & KNOWING
BOLD OBSERVATIONS

CHAPTER 4 -TRUSTING GOD & KNOWING
FINAL OBSERVATIONS & ACTIONS

CHAPTER 5

Speaking Things into Existence

"There is power in speaking people's names before the Lord.
When others hear someone talk to Jesus on their behalf,
healing often starts to take place."

— **Charles Stanley**

INSPIRATION

As Christians, our faith grows more and more each day. We begin this journey as babies desiring and longing for the milk of the Word. Scripture describes this phase as "like newborn babies, crave pure spiritual milk, so that by it you may grow up in your salvation, now that you have tasted that the Lord is good (1 Peter 2:2,3, NIV). This (a growing faith) happens through your Christian experiences and completing Christian-based studies. Both enable you to develop your faith enough to begin speaking things into existence. Simply put, to be able to speak things into existence, you first must believe.

Jesus wants us to follow him. He also wants us to be like him. The student is not above the teacher, but everyone who is fully trained will be like their teacher (Luke 6:40, NIV). He wants us to have the confidence in doing the same things that he did. See how Jesus explains it as written by the Apostle, Luke.

Very truly I tell you, whoever believes in me will do the works I have been doing, and they will do even greater things than these, because I am going to the Father. And I will do whatever you ask in my name, so that the Father may be glorified in the Son. You may ask me for anything in my name, and I will do it (Luke 14:12-14, NIV).

Once you hear God speak or before you begin to visualize things in your future, thank Him for what He is showing you. Praise Him in advance for what He is about to do because it is already done. Let God count you as righteous for believing Him. Honor God by calling those things which do not exist as though they did (Romans 4:17, NKJV). Let God know how much you love and trust Him. I know that He already knows because He is God but tell Him anyway. Why? Because He loves to be praised! So, praise Him for His mighty works and praise Him according to His excellent greatness. Rest assured that when you are thanking Him as I said earlier, you are praising Him!

The bible says, "See, the former things have taken place, and new things I declare; before they spring into being, I announce them to you" (Isaiah 42:9, NIV). "For it is with your heart that you believe and are justified, and it is with your mouth that you profess your faith and are saved" (Romans 10:10, NIV). The bible goes on to declare, "The tongue has the power of life and death, and those who love it will eat its fruit" (Proverbs 18:21, NIV).

At the outset of what we call time, God spoke things into existence (Genesis 1: 3, 24, 27 NIV). For example, when God wanted light, He called it forth and there it was. He did the same with wanting there to be living creatures in the water and birds in the sky. He even did it with man, by calling him into existence to resemble God and have dominion over the creatures in the sea, sky and on land.

As a child of God, by the power of the Holy Spirit that lives and works within, you, too, can speak things into existence just as your Father has. Ask according to His will, and you can have what you asked for. For instance, you may say, "Let there be resources, that I can return to college," and a grant surfaces. And you say, "Let there be someone that I can help today, and a stranger you meet at a convenience store asks that you pray for her. Here's another example; you may say, "I'm going to attend law school, pass the bar and in five years relocate to South Florida", and it comes to pass. Or you may say, "my son or daughter will be off drugs in the name of Jesus." Your son or daughter not only gets clean from drugs, but they also get married, buy a new home and own their own business." The point is that as long as it is His will, you can have what you asked for. God is awesome and he is spectacular.

The bible goes on to say, "Therefore I tell you, whatever you ask for in prayer, believe that you have received it, and it will be yours" (Mark 11:24, NIV). "Ask, and it will be given to you; seek and you will find; knock and the door will be opened to you (Matthew 7:7, NIV).

LIFE EXPERIENCE

I want to share an example of the power of speaking things into existence as I have witnessed people (including myself) do this on many occasions. This example happened in my life when I competed in sports. I had a football teammate whose name was Ivory

Smith. Ivory and I played together as teammates beginning in Neptune Pop Warner and then on to the Neptune High School football team in New Jersey. Ivory was a great athlete. I remember getting onto the team bus for an away game. As we sometimes did, Ivory and I sat together near the back of the team bus that would transport the team to Marlboro Township to play the Mustangs. On this cool crisp Saturday morning on the Jersey Shore, Ivory was much more talkative than normal. He always talked a lot but, on that day, he was really "psyched up" as we used to say. Now mind you, I had known Ivory for a long time, but I can remember thinking, *man, he is going off today*! He expressed emphatically the actions and strategies that we needed to execute to win the game. I agreed with him, however, in a subtler way. I mean, Ivory talked from the time that we left our high school until the time we arrived at the playing field, which took about 30 minutes. But here is the thing that Ivory said that I will never forget. I remember it like it was yesterday. He looked me straight in the eyes and said, "I'm telling you right now, I'm picking off (intercepting) two of them (passes) today, and I'm going in the end zone (scoring a touchdown) with one of them!! GAME OVER!! I'm talking about GAME Over"!! I have chills right now thinking about what he said as I'm writing it in this book. Those were his exact words, and he said it three or four times consecutively. "I'm telling you right now, I'm going to get two picks (interceptions) and I'm going in the end zone with one of them. I'm going to get two today and I'm going in the end zone with one of them. You watch! I'm telling you"! I'll tell you, he spoke that outcome into existence.

There was no doubt in his mind that he was going to do that on that day. Absolutely positively no doubt. Game OVER! So, we are playing the game. The Marlboro Township quarterback dropped back to pass and throws the ball in Ivory's direction. Ivory Smith swoops in, picks off the pass and starts streaking down the sideline towards the end zone. I was trying to get in front of him to block, but Ivory was so determined to do what he spoke into existence I couldn't catch up to him. I can remember running behind him and saying to myself, *isn't this something?* He said he was going to pick off two passes and score on one of them. And now, he is on his way to doing what he said he would do. When we got into the end zone, Ivory looked at me and said, "Didn't I tell you I was going in the end zone? I told you. I told you I was going into the end zone with at least one of them". Well you already know the rest, later in the game Ivory picked off another pass to complete the two interceptions that he spoke into existence on the team bus earlier that morning. With that, we went on to win the game. This was not a coincidence; nor was this luck. Getting two interceptions and returning one for a touchdown would normally be a difficult feat to say the least. Sometimes in life you just know. You don't even know how or why you know. You just do. On a crisp fall day many years ago, Ivory Smith surely knew, and I did, too! You have to call it what it is. I loved those days. I love my teammates and I love the memories. Thank you, God. We were all just 16 and 17-year-old kids at the time. So, as you can see, you do not have to be super spiritual to speak things into existence. Yet imagine how powerful you are when you do have a close and intimate connection with God. Oh, how much more He will do for you.

BIBLICAL EXAMPLE

There is no better example and lesson about speaking things into existence and faith than when God created the universe.

By faith we understand that the universe was created by the word of God, so that what is seen was not made of things that are visible (Hebrews 11:3 ESV)

65

From the very beginning God showed us that we could speak things into existence by faith that it will happen. By faith Abel offered to God a more acceptable sacrifice than Cain, through which he was commended as righteous, God commending him by accepting his gifts. And through his faith, though he died, he still speaks. By faith Enoch was taken up so that he should not see death, and he was not found, because God had taken him. Now before he was taken he was commended as having pleased God (Hebrews 11:5, ESV).

BOLD CONCLUSION

Jesus wanted the Disciples to have the confidence to do the things that He did, and to do even greater things than what He did when He was gone. You should be able to do greater things. If you shoot for the moon, at least you will land amongst the stars. Have you ever done something in your life that you really did not think that you would be able to do? Have you ever done something that you once thought never in your wildest imagination you would be able to do that? Don't think small; think big. You cannot be timid. Even when you are, you have to speak to yourself and say, 'I can do this through Christ who strengthens me'. After all, you are propelling the thing into motion with your trust in God that He will allow or make it happen. You are activating your faith that you can make it happen through God. You are executing the faith that God will make it happen because it lines up with His purpose.

The secular world is on to this as well. Barack Obama's "Yes we can" slogan was powerful. Nike's "Just Do It" campaign was bold, effective and powerful. They had to believe it for it to be successful. You cannot be afraid because God does not want you to be afraid. He wants bold confident soldiers on the battlefield to fight the good fight of faith and to win souls to Christ.

There is no time to waste. Activate the *Bold & Crazy Faith* that is in your spirit. Remember you have the One who is able to keep you from falling on your side. Keep going and talking about who God is. Even on a rainy day, He is your Bright and Morning Star. When things get ugly, know that you are the son or daughter of the Beautiful Rose of Sharon who got up to lift you up. He is all-powerful and capable of doing all things. He is not only capable of doing all things He is capable of doing all things well. Speak a thing and it shall come to pass. Believe it will be so, in the name of Jesus. Because you are saved by grace through your faith in God, you can call those things that be not as though they already are. Call into   existence those hopes and dreams that God clearly gave you a vision for. Do not be weak in your faith. Instead think big and think strong. You are a son and daughter of El Elyon, The Most High God.

CHAPTER 5 -SPEAKING THINGS INTO EXISTENCE
BOLD OBSERVATIONS

_____

_____

_____

_____

_____

_____

_____

_____

_____

_____

_____

_____

_____

_____

CHAPTER 5 -SPEAKING THINGS INTO EXISTENCE
BOLD OBSERVATIONS

_____

_____

_____

_____

_____

_____

_____

_____

_____

_____

_____

_____

_____

_____

CHAPTER 5 -SPEAKING THINGS INTO EXISTENCE
BOLD OBSERVATIONS

_____

_____

_____

_____

_____

_____

_____

_____

_____

_____

_____

_____

_____

_____

CHAPTER 5 -SPEAKING THINGS INTO EXISTENCE
BOLD OBSERVATIONS

CHAPTER 5 -SPEAKING THINGS INTO EXISTENCE
BOLD OBSERVATIONS

_____

_____

_____

_____

_____

_____

_____

_____

_____

_____

_____

_____

_____

_____

CHAPTER 5 -SPEAKING THINGS INTO EXISTENCE
FINAL OBSERVATION & ACTIONS

CHAPTER 6

Praising and Thanking God in Advance

"You can't get around pain and opposition, but you can try to be joyful in the trial... and thank God for the strength to get through it."

— **Mary J. Blige**

INSPIRATION

One of the most popular Christian sayings is "When praises go up, blessings come down." Although it is a catchy phrase and has a nice ring to it, I would go out on a limb and say that its popularity is rooted in truth. Support for this popular saying can be drawn from Psalms 22 (ASV). But what happens when we praise and thank God in advance, meaning before and during our trials and tribulation and before He delivers us out of these woes? What does thanking Him do for us, and what does it do for Him?

First, praising God and thanking Him in advance shows God that you trust him. It also demonstrates to God and displays to people that you have ultimate confidence in Him. He already knows our feelings. Still, praising and thanking Him in advance is confirmation that you have grown significantly and truly have an authentic relationship with Him. When the praise goes up, the blessings come down. Praising Him in good and bad times is crucial in your growth and development. In doing so, you are letting God know that your faith is bold. Even praising and thanking Him to allow negativity in your life to grow and develop your faith is bold. Praising God for what He has already done is good and easy. However, you need to have *Bold & Crazy Faith* to praise and thank God in advance for allowing negative situations into your life. Just knowing that He has the power to prevent negativity and still welcome it into your life takes your spiritual maturity to a higher level.

LIFE EXPERIENCE

A few years ago, I was seeking a promotion at my job with the federal government. Prior to the promotion, I had been in the same position for four or five years, a position that was not paying me adequately for the title, task and responsibilities that came with the position. In a nutshell, I was working in a position that had the duties and responsibilities that were two grades above my actual pay grade.

I want to make a note that I applied for this position even though it was well above my pay grade with the hopes that my hard work, skill and determination would set me apart for promotions that would be coming out eventually. You see, I felt that I was well-suited for this position because the duties were similar and somewhat aligned with jobs that I held in the private sector before working for the federal government. Further, the position would allow me to use my strong attributes of excellent communication, networking and persuasion. I felt that once I accomplished the requirements of the job, my leadership skills, work ethic and the favor of God would set me apart eventually. The program that I managed was very large, very active, and highly visible across the globe. I did an excellent job for years in this position as evidenced by my annual evaluations and the availability of monies for funding due to my planning, programming, and coordination in the budgeting and the execution for the programs to move forward in their lifecycles. After years went by, and it became evident that I was not going to get a promotion in that position, I decided that a change needed to happen. Even writing this book takes *Bold & Crazy Faith* as some people that read this may not understand and try to hold me back, but I am not worried about it because I know that promotion and elevation comes from the north (God). God will intercede and orchestrate on your behalf everything that He needs, to place you where He wants you. In time, I asked my boss for a reassignment stating all the reasons that made sense.

My request for a reassignment was granted, and I was ready for a new beginning. It was not a pay raise or promotion, just a lateral reassignment in the same position with a different division and program within the same organization. Understand this! Know when the writing is on the wall, and therefore be expeditious in making a change when you know that this is the case. Listen to God when He is telling you that a chapter in your life is over. Sometimes you will know that you are in a position in life that a door has shut to the point of no return. Recognize it and take the faithful actions to move forward and away from it. Do not think that this situation or circumstance has happened to destroy you, shut you down, or harm you. Rather, know that sometimes God is moving you out of a situation to help you and promote you to His next assignment and position. God will be the catalyst behind it all because He wants you to shift in his direction and in your life. He really is in control, though He gives you free will to make your own decisions. The key is in this question: are you making your decisions based on His direction?

Even before I presented my request for reassignment, I made a conscious decision to turn back to my spiritual foundation and devotional relationship with God. In all honesty, it was out of desperation. You see, I was having devotional time inconsistently during the day, sometimes intentionally and sometimes unintentionally—meaning worship happened in my spare time or out of guilt or duty. Let me explain. I would sometimes have two or three good days and then sometimes squeeze it in for God in the mornings. But now I was having devotion intentionally on a regular, reoccurring daily basis. For me, it really is not good enough to have devotion daily with God at different times of the day because that is not a part of His and my covenant. It's just not, and I know it. Sometimes I still fall short with devotion in the morning. You and I know that when you are desperate and need something from God, you will find time for Him. The point is to stay consistent on a regular basis, even when you are not asking or needing God for something desperately. Don't 'pimp' God. That is, do not come to him or spend time with him only when you need something. He should hear from you regularly.

Bold & Crazy Faith is praising Him in advance before you see the outcome of what He has already done, which is yet to be manifested. You are ready to walk into your future that God has already prepared. Some people do not understand this. Life can get so hard that you sometimes need to encourage yourself with what you already know by faith. Sometimes it comes out in your attitude or personality and people mistake it for arrogance, cockiness or brashness. They try to get you upset. They try to make you miserable because they do not understand why you still hold the same positive attitude and boldness that you had from the beginning. They have noticed your unshakable character and are intimidated by it. More specifically, they are really taking offense to the confidence that you have in your Lord and Savior Jesus Christ. You don't even have to broadcast your beliefs in the workplace; yet they sense that there is something different about you. Yes, there is. Faith! *Bold & Crazy Faith*!!

I began to spend time with God in prayer every morning while driving into work. I would pray for my wife, daughter, siblings, in-laws, extended family, pastor and first family, the diaconate, church, supervisors, bosses, and co-workers. I would also pray for anything or anyone that came to mind at that time and sometimes for myself.

Upon my 6:00AM arrival at work, I would start my computer. Enjoying my coffee in the quiet and while it was booting up, I would read my daily devotional. My devotional read took all of two to five minutes, the amount of time that it takes for my computer to boot. After reading my devotional and with my computer ready to go, I would check my email that came after I left work from the day prior. After checking and answering any emails that needed a reply, I would take a brisk walk around the huge building. The building would be quiet because mostly everyone had not arrived for the day yet. I would sometimes listen to gospel music on my headphones while walking to focus on God, what He was saying and directing me to do. Doing this daily was not only enjoyable, it was also very effective. My daily routine of spending time with God early in the morning provided peace and clarity. It also increased my faith to implement the steps that I needed to move forward.

Every Christian has a unique relationship with God. For me, the intimacy of my relationship with the Lord usually takes place early in the morning. This is the time that I best hear from Him, and this is the time that I feel that He is clearly listening to me. Now this is not absolute, as I have heard from God at different times of the day in my life. I know that He is always with me and able to hear me at all times. However, in the morning it sometimes feels more like a conversation between the two of us. Don't get me wrong. There were times that I let doubt seep in. At those times, I looked at God's track record in my life to remember the same feelings and processes (devotion, praise and thanksgiving) to know the outcome will be the same as before. Victory! Blessings! I know that because He did it before, He will do it again. God was the one who got me the job in the first place. God blessed me with the job and provided for my wife and I to relocate to Maryland, where each of us would receive a great federal job. God granted my prayer request to take the lateral reassignment. He may not do it the same way, but He will work in your favor again, again and again. When we have that time together, I am assured and know on a higher level that whatever I am trusting God for or working out, it is only a matter of time that I will experience breakthrough. So I praise Him and thank Him in advance for what He has already done, although the outcome has not surfaced in the physical—*yet*. I sometimes thank Him in the moment of the prayer or in the middle of my request. As for you, you can thank Him before the manifestation in your life, exercising your boldness and trust that He has already worked it out.

My reassignment was granted. I vowed to God that I would keep the same devotional time knowing that it was the catalyst for my reassignment and that the reassignment would put me in a better position for promotion. I told God and myself that I would not get too busy or prioritize my job over him and not spend quality time with him first thing in the morning. After being reassigned, I received a promotion in under six months. My promotion came outside my organization with the federal government and the pay plan classified me two pay grades above what I had been. God made up for the two pay grades in one shot when conventionally I would have had to get two promotions to move up two pay grades. Though I was not expecting that, God Himself will far exceed the expectations that you have and will bless you exceedingly just like the bible says He will. One year later, I was qualified for another promotion that I am praising and thanking God for in advance. Thank you, God, for this promotion. It has not happened yet, but right now I am praising and thanking you for it because I know that it is already done. I PRAISE YOU for promotion! That is *Bold &Crazy Faith*! That is Praising and Thanking God in advance. That is Trusting God. The proof is in the pudding. I will be giving a praise report on this when it manifests in the physical. Let everything that has breath praise the Lord!

BIBLICAL EXAMPLE

A **Song of Praise for the LORD's Faithfulness to His People**

A Psalm of Thanksgiving

(Psalm 100:1-5, NJKV)

Make a joyful shout to the LORD, all you lands!
Serve the LORD with gladness;
Come before His presence with singing.
Know that the LORD, He *is* God;
It is He *who* has made us, and]not we ourselves;
We are His people and the sheep of His pasture.

Enter into His gates with thanksgiving,
And into His courts with praise.
Be thankful to Him, *and* bless His name.
For the LORD *is* good;
His mercy *is* everlasting,
And His truth *endures* to all generations.

BOLD CONCLUSION

If you really want to please God, begin to praise him and thank him in advance today. Not only will this be pleasing to Him, but you will also gain a new boldness that will steadily build over time. As God continually blesses you as the result of His faithfulness, your faith will increase by the bold trust that you have in Him. God will reward the *Bold & Crazy Faith* that you have in Him again, again, and again. The blessings that the Lord is going to pour out on you will sometimes be mind-boggling. For example, there will be times that the turnaround time for your answered prayer will be instant.

As an ambassador for Christ, there is no excuse not to be one of the biggest cheerleaders for Our Lord and Savior. He IS the one who is able to keep you from falling. If you want to be close to God, you should praise Him in good times and in bad times. Even when you get a bad report, praise Him in advance because you trust that He has already worked it out. Life may present a roadblock. Nevertheless, praise God because you know that the roadblock is just temporary. People may try to throw a wrench in your game plan. But, praise God in advance and thank Him for the knowledge of knowing no person can overthrow God's game plan that He has designed for you and only you. Hallelujah!

CHAPTER 6 -PRAISING & THANKING GOD IN ADVANCE
BOLD OBSERVATIONS

CHAPTER 6 -PRAISING & THANKING GOD IN ADVANCE
BOLD OBSERVATIONS

_____

_____

_____

_____

_____

_____

_____

_____

_____

_____

_____

_____

_____

_____

CHAPTER 6 -PRAISING & THANKING GOD IN ADVANCE
BOLD OBSERVATIONS

_____

_____

_____

_____

_____

_____

_____

_____

_____

_____

_____

_____

_____

CHAPTER 6 -PRAISING & THANKING GOD IN ADVANCE
BOLD OBSERVATIONS

_____

_____

_____

_____

_____

_____

_____

_____

_____

_____

_____

_____

_____

CHAPTER 6 -PRAISING & THANKING GOD IN ADVANCE
BOLD OBSERVATIONS

CHAPTER 6 -PRAISING & THANKING GOD IN ADVANCE
FINAL OBSERVATIONS & ACTIONS

CHAPTER 7

Now That You Are off to the Races

"There are some people that look at faith as a part of their life, and there are those like me that look at faith as the essence of their life. I look at all things through my faith."

— **Roland Martin**

INSPIRATION

Now that you are off to the races, you likely find that the joy of being a Christian is exhilarating. You have experienced the super natural power of God first-hand and in the lives of others. The wonder-working power of Jesus Christ is real and is in full effect. People that you know are being healed from illnesses that should have taken them out. Others are being delivered from drugs and alcohol. There are friends and family members who are getting married when you and they themselves thought that they were not marriage material. Yes indeed, Our God is alive forever-more. Additionally, since the time you began this journey, you have experienced God opening doors for you that you knew would not have opened had it not been for the Lord on your side. You have met people that you would have never met and been places that you would have never been. There are people that you have met since beginning this walk that were directly sent by God. God sent them to be major blessings and difference-makers in your life. "Oh yes, He is the Great Orchestrator!" Whether it was meant for a season or forever, they were sent to be influencers in your life.

One of the many things God does is expand your territory. In order for Him to get you to where He needs you to be, He will arrange and orchestrate introductions for you. He will introduce you to people, places and things. He wants you to see more, be more and experience more. God knows that you need to grow and develop, to carry out the purposes that He has for your life. He knows that when you are encouraged by others, you gain an attitude and the confidence of *yes, I can do this*. When God expands your territory, he will provide you the means to see and experience other places and how people live differently than you. He will provide you access to various cultures and processes that broaden your horizons. When God expands your territory and broadens your horizons, you will experience the joy of trying something new. As a result of the expansion from all the new possibilities, your faith increases dramatically. You take on an excitement, vigor and shift in your mindset as it relates to how you look at your circumstances. Instead of giving into despair, you think, *Ah, hah! I really "can do all things through Christ who strengthens me" (Philippians 4:13, NKJV)*.

It is in these times that you need to capitalize on God being active in your life. Take full advantage in what God is showing you and exposing you to. Use the momentum to catapult you into more of God's blessings. When you are in your season of expansion and overflow, stay locked in with God as he will move things along expeditiously and bless you exponentially. You will have personal experiences with receiving blessings. Blessings after blessings!

Blessings of health and blessings of wealth. The benefits and blessings of your Christian journey and lifestyle will really begin to sink in. You will realize that this Christian lifestyle is what's UP! Following Jesus is the best and most effective way to live life and maximize your potential. Getting to meet new and interesting people is what's up. Being positively open minded and trying new things is what's up. Traveling to new places and seeing how things are done elsewhere is what's up. Living a clean life for God and my family is what's up. It is in this growth and development that you continually learn that there is no limit to what God can do and no limit to what you can do through Him. Even if you are not wealthy according to the world's narrow standard of wealthy, you will be wealthy with peace, wisdom, understanding and knowledge. You will gain a true understanding of overflow. Capture a snapshot and remember these times, for later in your faith walk, you will need to draw from these memories for strength and endurance. I'll talk about that later in Chapter 10, Boldness in God's Silence. During those times, just remember. He is more than able!

This Christian life is sensational and very rewarding. Yet, the reality and truth to this lifestyle is the understanding that the good times will not last forever. The journey will not be peaches and cream in its entirety. You will experience the highs and lows. It will take a certain level of maturity in much the same way as we described in Chapter 5, "Praising and Thanking God in Advance" to balance the highs and lows. The key is knowing that the lows are designed to strengthen you and provide growth and spiritual muscle to win tough battles that are on the horizon. The lows also provide a reference point in your spiritual memory to help you in the difficult times that are surely coming. It is in these times that a *Bold & Crazy Faith* is developed.

As a Christian you will experience valley moments and seasons where you will be tested often. Sometimes you will just have to seek God while you are in your valley or test. I will refer to this again in Chapter 10 where I discuss Boldness in God's Silence. At any rate, do not become discouraged. The bible says, "Consider it pure joy, my brothers and sisters, whenever you face trials of many kinds, because you know that the testing of your faith produces perseverance. ⁴Let perseverance finish its work so that you may be mature and complete, not lacking anything" (James 1:2-4 NIV). Though you may be tried in the fire, you will come out as pure gold. Your faith is far more precious than even gold.

Talk to leaders and your peers in your church about their experiences. Keep learning, keep seeking, keep pushing. Attend church on a regular basis and get connected to a ministry that uses the gifts that God gave you. Fellowship is a major benefit of being a member of the church as there is strength in having an extended family. Being around like-minded people of faith will help inspire you to want to be in God's presence often.

LIFE EXPERIENCE

The Christian journey is like a marathon. As described earlier this race, is complete with ups and downs and twists and turns. This race is not a sprint, so you need to pace yourself accordingly to win the race. And similar to the outcome of running a marathon, victory is assured—*only* if you stay the course. You see in a marathon it's not as much about winning the race but finishing the race. In the Christian life, if you finish you win. Not only is this journey a race but it is also a fight. A fight to the finish. Fight the good fight of the faith. The bible says, "Fight the good fight of the faith. Take hold of the eternal life to which you were called when you made your good confession in the presence of many witnesses" (1 Timothy 6:12 NIV). Furthermore in this passage, Paul goes on to say, "I have fought the good fight, I have finished the race, I have kept the faith. Now there is in store for me the crown of righteousness, which the Lord, the righteous Judge, will award to me on that day—and not only to me, but also to all who have longed for his appearing. (2 Timothy 4:7,8 NIV).

Know this – there will be times that you will need to fight. Not a physical fight but a spiritual one. There will be people that will come up against you and you will ask yourself, *what did I do to them?* The attacks are not because of actions that you have taken against them. They are about your connection with Christ. If the saying misery loves company is true, then unhappy people will be very bothered by your peace and blessings. They may even become envious of you for having that or exuding that. What they don't understand is that you have your own drama going on. However, you choose not to wear it on your sleeve because you have the bold faith that whatever it is that you are dealing with will eventually pass or be worked out. A mature Christian realizes that troubles do always come; however a problem is resolved in one way or other. Further, a strong, mature Christian also knows that these things come with the territory of being a representative for Christ.

The rewards are spectacular. God will truly bless you beyond belief. I can remember getting the opportunity to travel on business to Germany. Many people in my organization put in for the opportunity to go, and I was selected. This was not an ordinary Temporary Duty (TDY) as we call it among federal agencies. This was TDY for one month to a great location. Our place of duty was at Grafenwoehr, Germany; however, while we were there, we stayed in a quaint city called Amberg. Amberg was a small village built with a wall around its exterior. It had a medieval yet contemporary feel to it. Our team also had the opportunity to visit Prague and other areas in Europe such as the Czech Republic and Amsterdam. We also visited other areas of Germany to include Frankfurt, Nuremberg, Mannheim and Munich. Who would have ever thought that I would have a chance to go to Amberg, Germany on business? Who would have ever thought that I would have the opportunity to visit Munich where I had childhood memories of the Munich Olympiad and the chaos that surrounded the games in 1972? I got the chance to walk those same streets that were once disrupted by violence. We received a tour of Munich by one of my co-worker's family who lived there. I had the opportunity to see some of the most breathtaking church edifices in the world. God is awesome!

Every Sunday while I was in Germany, I tuned in to our live streaming worship service at The New Psalmist Baptist Church in Baltimore, MD. On the first Sunday that I was in Amberg, Germany watching and listening to my pastor Bishop Walter Scott Thomas Sr., he preached a sermon that was so relevant and dead-on to what I was feeling and experiencing at that time. Bishop Thomas preached about how so many people in our congregation had been blessed above and beyond what most of us ever thought was possible. He said, "some of you have been so blessed that you now have high-powered jobs that fly you across the country and all around the world". He went deeper and said, "Imagine the level of trust that your employer needs to have in you for that kind of responsibility." I lost it, right there in my Hotel room in Amberg!! I began jumping up and down and praising God at the top of my voice," THANK YOU, LORD"!! I remembered thinking for a second that the other guests might hear me, but I didn't care because I was that blessed, and I knew it. I had been thinking the same thing since my selection for the assignment, packing to leave, upon my arrival to Germany and during that broadcast. I was tripping out on the whole experience. I can remember thinking I almost can't believe this. I am on the other side of the world, sitting in a beautiful hotel room, in a beautiful city, in Germany for one whole month, drinking some of the best expresso and cappuccino that the world has to offer, on business, watching our church service on a computer and my pastor is Bishop Walter Scott Thomas Sr. I remember thinking, *it doesn't get any better than this.* But it does!

BIBLICAL EXAMPLE

The prophet Jeremiah faced stiff competition. Eventually, he got so despondent that he asked God, "why does the way of the wicked prosper (Jeremiah 12:1, NIV)?" Just think, we are talking about a prophet asking God why bad people live at ease. Jeremiah had to compete against ruthless priests and idolaters that came up against him. He questioned why the wicked were happy and always seemed to prosper. In His response to Jeremiah's laments, God cuts to the chase. He questions Jeremiah's ability to handle the big stuff that is surely coming his way, if he couldn't handle the small stuff first—like watching other people advance while he wasn't. In essence, what Jeremiah was looking at was just peanuts compared to storms that will be raging in his life eventually. The same is true for you.

God promised Jeremiah that all of the wicked including the people of Judah will be uprooted from their respective properties. But after He uproots them, He will show them compassion and restore them back to their inheritance and their own country. God also told Jeremiah and warned that they needed to learn to acknowledge Him as Lord to be reestablished among His people.

BOLD CONCLUSION

If God has empowered you to run with horses, there is no need to sweat the small stuff. When you are off to the races and living in the will of God, there is no person or entity that can prevent you from fulfilling the purposes that God has for you. No matter what, be bold in your faith! Know this: you are a like horse built with endurance to run among the other horses. You are built for the long haul.

So now that you are off to the races, be BOLD my brother, and be BOLD my sister. He has given you everything that you need and more to have the victory!

CHAPTER 7 -NOW THAT YOU ARE OFF TO THE RACES
BOLD OBSERVATIONS

CHAPTER 7 -NOW THAT YOU ARE OFF TO THE RACES
BOLD OBSERVATIONS

_____

_____

_____

_____

_____

_____

_____

_____

_____

_____

_____

_____

_____

CHAPTER 7 -NOW THAT YOU ARE OFF TO THE RACES
BOLD OBSERVATIONS

CHAPTER 7 -NOW THAT YOU ARE OFF TO THE RACES
BOLD OBSERVATIONS

_____

_____

_____

_____

_____

_____

_____

_____

_____

_____

_____

_____

_____

_____

_____

_____

CHAPTER 7 -NOW THAT YOU ARE OFF TO THE RACES
BOLD OBSERVATIONS

CHAPTER 7 -NOW THAT YOU ARE OFF TO THE RACES
FINAL OBSERVATIONS & ACTIONS

_____

_____

_____

_____

_____

_____

_____

_____

_____

_____

_____

_____

_____

_____

_____

CHAPTER 8

Facing the Enemy

"One of Satan's most deceptive and powerful ways of defeating us is to get us to believe a lie. And the biggest lie is that there are no consequences to our own doing. Satan will give you whatever you ask for if it will lead you where he ultimately wants you."

— **Charles Stanley**

INSPIRATION

To have *Bold & Crazy Faith* you need an understanding of why and how Satan attacks. This is one of the most important areas to understand for effective Christian living. Understanding this is vital.

First, know that Satan is real, but also take heart in knowing that Jesus has your covered. Jesus has your back, front, side and your middle. He really does have you covered from the top of your head to the souls of your feet. The bible declares, "the thief comes only to steal and kill and destroy; I have come that they may have life and have it to the full" (John10:10, NIV). Realize that the devil is not happy about your relationship with God. He will try anything that he can to destroy your relationship with Him and stop you from having an effect in the Kingdom of God. Don't let him steal, kill or destroy your boldness! Remember, "no weapon forged against you will prevail (Isaiah 54:17 NIV).

Prepare and learn to recognize attacks from the enemy. The bible teaches us and gives us many examples of Satan and his devices and there are many books that have been written to help you understand how the devil attacks. I recommend that you take the time to dive into this subject much deeper in your own time as it is a spiritual investment that will pay off undoubtedly. The more you know about the enemy will allow you to anticipate some attacks before they even happen. Preparation and anticipation is key. When you are prepared for an attack you can proceed in your faith with a boldness that just increases over time. There is a saying that I heard years ago in the Christian community that still holds true, "If the devil is not on your trail then you are not making any waves.

Next, know that you are on the right track when the devil rears his ugly head. The devil will always make a last-ditch effort to stamp out any success that you will have that will make a difference in the Kingdom. But always remember this, "The devil is a liar." Even as I write the words on this page the devil has tried to remind me about things in my past or tell me "Are you really qualified to write this book." All nonsense! He knows that I am qualified. He knows that my mission as an inspirational writer is to motivate people who are stagnant, stuck, hopeless or broken. I inspire people through knowledge, life experiences and witnessing to the love, power and saving grace of our Lord and Savior Jesus Christ. He knows that for some, this book will be life changing. The devil knows that this book will be a game changer for you and me.

As you grow in your Christian experience you will begin to recognize that Satan will tempt you to do things that are not pleasing to God. Especially at times that you are about to make a break through or accomplish something substantial. He is always working but he works extra hard to discourage you right before the break through. I like to call him the "Great Hater". He wants to cause misery in your life, and you know that misery loves company. Satan would love for you to commit sin after sin. The bible says, "No, in all these things we are more than conquerors through him who loved us (Romans 8:37, NIV).

When the devil tries to rise up in your life with the intent to steal, kill and destroy you speak the word of God over your life and make it personal. My bible teaches me, "the one who is in you is greater than the one who is in the world (John 4:4 NIV)!! I command you to back up in the name of Jesus. Speak life and victory over yourself and your situation. Psalm 23. Prepares a table in the presence of my enemies. Command resurrection of the situation that he has tried to steal. Command resurrection over the situation that he has tried to kill. Command resurrection over the situation that he has tried to   destroy. This is not an exhaustive lesson on the subject. Much of what you will learn about in dealing with and defeating the enemies' attacks will come from your own experiences. I am reminded of a phrase that the sorority Alpha Kappa Alpha uses, as I am thinking of a way to describe going head up with the Enemy. "This is a serious matter." Be prepared, for this is a serious matter.

Let's face it, in the perfect world you would always be prepared for an attack from the enemy. However, we know that the world is not perfect, and our lives are far from it. Therefore, let me give you a few tidbits to help you recognize attacks from Satan.

When things happen in your life that makes absolutely no sense. I'm not talking about things that don't seem to make any sense I'm talking about things that make absolutely no kind of sense. They can sometimes be described as very trivial or the most trivial things. When there are once-in-a-lifetime type of negative situations that arise is also another sign of the enemy. Remember this because it is key. These occurrences always happen right before you have a great blessing or celebration of some sort or they happen right after you receive great news of promotion, elevation or celebration. It's weird but it really is predictable. It's so crazy because when you are caught up, it catches you off guard. You will find yourself getting upset that you allowed Satan to slip one past you and annoyed at yourself that you were not prepared to recognize that an attack was coming before it even happened. Life has a way of keeping us engrossed so much to a point that we lose our spiritual bearings and let our guards down. Satan slips in like a thief in the night and tries to snuff you out.

As I hinted above, another way to tell that you are under attack is the extreme tone that is being used that really is not necessary for the situation at hand. Sometimes an attack is so crazy that you can see and feel the presence of an evil spirit that is so thick you can't believe that the people around you cannot sense the truth of what is really happening. Sometimes with people their attitude and countenance are so different and so far from their regular self that it is like looking evil right in the eye. It really is amazing. One of the most common ways that Satan works is through people. Additionally, the devil will work through your weaknesses. I like to think of it as the low hanging poison. Once he knows that you are not going to fail in that area he will move on to another area. Never underestimate Satan or the extent that he will go to destroy you. He is very conniving and crafty. For our struggle is not against flesh and blood, but against the rulers, against the authorities, against the powers of this dark world and against the spiritual forces of evil in the heavenly realms (Ephesians 6:12, NIV).

LIFE EXPERIENCE

In your walk with Christ there will be many attacks. Satan will send fiery darts in the form of lies and negative words from people that you least expect. The devil will try to throw a wrench into great relationships that you have by causing misunderstandings to surface just as your needs are being met or productivity is taking place. Satan will cause illness to overtake your body and put you down just as an opportunity arises. Your car may break down on the day of your big interview. Mayhem may erupt in your household with your spouse and children.

As I reminisce over my life, I am reminded of the many times that I was under attack with the devil. Most of the time the attack was over something as simple as words that were misinterpreted in a conversation or a lack of communication that senselessly got out of hand. On many occasions I have sensed an attack coming and commanded the devil to back up in the name of Jesus. I have declared silently and out loud that no weapon formed against me shall prosper. When you prepare for an attack because of receiving blessing let the devil know verbally in advance that you know that he will try to steal your joy, but you are not going to let that happen because God said it in his word that He would never leave me nor forsake me. If you are a new Christian it may seem weird to verbalize these declarations and commands however remember that life and death is in the power of the tongue. Speak life over your own situation and speak the word of God because the word is the truth.

BIBLICAL EXAMPLE

Job had *Bold & Crazy Faith*. How do you think he was able to endure a magnitude of rejection, persecution and physical suffering at the hands of family, friends and God? God asked Satan, have you considered my son Job and described the positive characteristics and attributes that Job had as a faithful man. There have been so many times that I have either read the story or heard the story of Job preached. I often wonder. Could I endure that type of humiliation? Probably not.

BOLD CONCLUSION

You will be persecuted because you are a Christian. Oh yes, it comes with the territory. Our Lord and Savior Jesus Christ suffered persecution on a regular basis. In fact, Jesus suffered the ultimate persecution which was crucifixion on the cross. Similarly, you will have to endure many humiliations in life. If you are born again, there is no doubt that you have already been.

Now that you are armed with the knowledge of how and why the devil attacks you, you will no longer fear making an impact in the lives of others. Satan knows that you will a make a significant difference in the lives of many people. He already knows that you will be blessed tremendously through the reading of this book. The enemy wants to extinguish the fire and drive that you need to be super productive. He wants to sniff out all your positive associations to divide you from your good relationships and damage the very fabric that holds them together. The devil wants to divide and conquer your relationships.

Satan already knows, that because of this book, you will obtain a vigor that will make you bolder on the battlefield. As a seasoned Christian, you will obtain a renewed boldness that is vital in overcoming lingering doubt. You will also develop the ability to recognize the attacks of the enemy and to distinguish these attacks from common negative occurrences that just happen in life.

Be bold, be bold, be bold and be ready! Well, how do you get ready? The Apostle Paul describes in Ephesians 6:10-18 that you need to put on the full armor of God, so that you can stand firmly against the devil's schemes. To help you understand the full armor of God, Paul describes armor that Roman soldiers used as a metaphor for the armor that you have as a Christian. He assures you that your battles are not against people but are against the spiritual attacks of Satan.

God wants you to stand firm with the belt of truth, buckled around your waist which means he wants you live in your commitment, in the truth of the gospel and the promises of God. He also wants you to stand firm with the breastplate of righteousness in place, meaning that your actions line up according to what God has said, pleasing God and showing the enemy that you will live according to the standards that God has set forth.

The Apostle Paul describes having your feet fitted with the readiness that comes from the gospel of peace. This is to say you are to practice asking God to confirm situations in your life by giving you peace. When there is discomfort associated with this, do not move forward. Additionally, you are to take up the shield of faith to extinguish all the flaming arrows of the evil one. In doing so, you are believing God is telling you the truth.

Ask God to support you in your actions, especially if those actions are hard to take. He wants you to take the helmet of salvation which means to control your thoughts and win the spiritual battle that is going on in your mind. You need to use the word of God that has renewed and transformed your thoughts as leverage to hold more weight in your mind then what the enemy has to say about anything.

Also, you need to take the sword of the Spirit, which is the word of God. Paul says, to pray in the Spirit on all occasions with all kinds of prayers and requests and be alert, praying for all the Lord's people. You need to bring in prayer and pray often as prayer is God's means of communicating from heaven to earth so that eternity enters time when you are under spiritual attack.

You now have the knowledge and tools to stand your ground and fight the spiritual fight to deter the enemy's mission to steal, kill and destroy. With the knowledge and tools to fight, you can be bold when Satan launches attacks. You are empowered to fight back spiritually and have the *Bold & Crazy Faith* to know that no weapon formed against you will prosper!

CHAPTER 8 -FACING THE ENEMY
BOLD OBSERVATIONS

CHAPTER 8 -FACING THE ENEMY
BOLD OBSERVATIONS

CHAPTER 8 -FACING THE ENEMY
BOLD OBSERVATIONS

CHAPTER 8 -FACING THE ENEMY
BOLD OBSERVATIONS

_____

_____

_____

_____

_____

_____

_____

_____

_____

_____

_____

_____

_____

CHAPTER 8 -FACING THE ENEMY
BOLD OBSERVATIONS

CHAPTER 8 -FACING THE ENEMY
FINAL OBSERVATIONS & ACTIONS

CHAPTER 9

Boldness in Your Witness

"Each game is an opportunity to be on a great stage and be a witness for Christ. When I step on the floor, people should know who I represent, who I believe in."

— **Stephen Curry**

INSPIRATION

Jesus wants us to share the good news of salvation and His love. He wants us to tell everybody about Him. A prerequisite to your bold stance for God is having the *Bold & Crazy Faith* that Jesus wants you to have to fulfill the instruction that he has given all Christians. When you are obedient, God rewards you like any proud father would with his children. Although the reward does not always happen at the time of our obedience, you will be rewarded. It may be at the restaurant when someone anonymously pays it forward by picking up your tab for lunch. Your reward may even come in the form of your son or daughter getting accepted into the college of his or her choice. Remember that your children will be blessed as a result of your faithfulness and obedience. The bible states, "Let us not become weary in doing good, for at the proper time we will reap a harvest if we do not give up" (Galatians 6:9, NIV).

We are sons and daughters of God. If you are a son or daughter of the Most High God, why shouldn't you have *Bold & Crazy Faith*? You should have *Bold & Crazy Faith* in your walk and *Bold & Crazy Faith* in your talk. That *Bold & Crazy Faith* in your talk should be in glorifying Him. Your *Bold & Crazy Faith* in your talk should be in obedience to Him. The boldness that you exude in witnessing is not supposed to come off as brash or arrogant, however; it should be very confident. Your boldness, when witnessing about the goodness of Jesus and the quality of your Christian lifestyle, should be more confident than a non-believer who is attempting to inspire someone about having a life of privilege according to the world's standards of successful living.

LIFE EXPERIENCE

The way in which you live your life is the most authentic way to witness. I am sure that you have heard the cliché, "actions speak louder than words." There is certainly truth to that. There is no better example of how the Christian life is supposed to be lived than by someone who is actively living the life. As I said before having a bold witness should reflect your confidence and experience in victorious living with God.

When it comes to intentional witnessing to others, your confidence and the help of the Holy Spirit will assist you in your cause for Christ. With the help of the Spirit, you will be bold and persuasive in your witness. Think about one or two of the best sales representatives that you have purchased goods or services from in the past. Why did you purchase from them? Most people purchase from peo-ple that they like but they also purchase from people that have knowledge in the product or service that they are interested in. You won't usually just buy from someone because you like them. Atleast not anything substantial. Most likely, you will buy from someone that knows what they are talking about and someone that is personable. Some of the best sales professionals present so well that you never think that they are trying to sell you. Well, it's similar when witnessing only you have the help of the Spirit.

The following is just one example of how you could witness your faith to another person.

I want to share the beauty of God's love with you. "Your witness should be one of, "you are missing out on one of the greatest things that you can ever possibly be a part of." If you only knew what I know. I know from experience that my life has not been the same since I started rolling with Jesus. Not even remotely close. I know from experience that the doors opened for me would never have happened had it not been for the Lord on my side."

Your *Bold & Crazy Faith* can be subtle yet consistent. Non evasive. You should always look for opportunity without being overbearing.

The change in my life was drastic. I'll put it like this. Jesus really did a number on me. For a very long time I was walking around and living my life and not knowing that this Jesus was always there and very present even though it did not seem like it. I cannot believe that I lived all those years in my own power when there was a God who was capable of helping me and supporting me through everything. I really wished that I would have listened when friends and family had told me earlier. Following Jesus Christ is what's up. I'm telling you because It would not be right to withhold the best thing that ever happened to me and so many other people that I know.

Your bold witness can also be evident by the way that you live your life. How you go about things. Or the way that you handle adversity. How do you generally respond? In other words, your response should not represent a state of desperation, devastation or finality. However, adversity should be viewed and handled as a temporary set-back or predicament that will eventually become favorable. It doesn't really matter if the predicament itself changes. You know that you will ultimately overcome or be delivered because of your relationship with God and the victory that you have in Him.

For starters in witnessing to others about Christ, begin with your own life experiences. When you testify in this manner, you set the stage for a before and after scenario. That is, discuss your life before salvation and after. In my case, when I surrendered my life it was not like going to prison; it was more like getting out of prison. Many people think that when they choose Christ, they are choosing restricted living; however, they are choosing an expansion in their living. In other words, by choosing Christ, they've chosen to upgrade their living. Who does not want an upgrade? An upgrade is a transformation that takes place in the way you think, expect and live. You now have a new depth of peace and freedom to think expansively and believe that your vision and thoughts will eventually translate into abundant living. Who the Son sets free is free indeed (John 8:36, NIV).

BIBLICAL EXAMPLE

With what is generally called The Great Commission, Jesus commanded his disciples to spread the gospel throughout the world.

Then the eleven disciples went to Galilee, to the mountain where Jesus had told them to go. When they saw him, they worshiped him; but some doubted. Then Jesus came to them and said,

"All authority in heaven and on earth has been given to me. Therefore go and make disciples of all nations, baptizing them in the name of the Father and of the Son and of the Holy Spirit, and teaching them to obey everything I have commanded you. And surely I am with you always, to the very end of the age" (Matthew 28:16-20, NIV).

BOLD CONCLUSION

This Christian journey is a process where you are always striving to get better despite knowing that you will never truly arrive at perfection. There are many people out there who believe that they do not have what it takes to be a Christian or to be saved. They think they have to get themselves together before they come to God or Christianity because there is this model of what a Christian is supposed to look like. Well whatever that model is supposed to look like it is likely flawed because we all are. It is your place to let people know that they will get better with time. No matter what their needs are they will be met by the love and power of OUR SOON and COMING KING. Be transparent with those that you are witnessing to. Share with them a few things that you are still boldly trusting God for. In the same way, explain that you fully expect He will work them out the same way he did with so many things in the past.

Only God is perfect. Yet, we strive for excellence. The bible says, we "press on toward the goal to win the prize for which God has called [us] heavenward in Christ Jesus" (Philippians 3:14, NIV).

As you are in Christ, old things are passed away and new things emerge. Some old things are gone immediately while others take time to dissipate. God works things out in each of us, according to the purposes that he uniquely has for us according to his overall purposes. In the order of salvation, there is a process you journey through called sanctification. As you grow as a Christian, you become holier in your walk with Christ. You are sanctified by the truth of God's word. So, you will continue to make mistakes as you develop but the difference is you now have a Savior who intercedes on your behalf and will be with you forever. Before living in Christ and living for Christ it is was as though you were traveling through life in coach. Now, as long as you are in Christ and Christ is in you, you are living first class. In the end, all of us have to "set [our] minds on things above, not on earthly things" (Colossians 3:2, NIV).

The key to having boldness in your witness is simple and not deep. Have the confidence that they will get you. They will understand you enough to know where you are coming from and the point that you are making. Talk about the applications that you have applied since receiving salvation and the results. When you are bold enough to share the things of God, your faith will increase. This is called authentic testimony. Some have observed or heard of your transformation and growth. Point to God and explain your willingness to change your lifestyle. Always glorify God as He is the author and finisher of your faith.

Some of the people who are around you on a regular basis have a need to know that Jesus really is a healer. Share with them how the Lord healed you or someone that you know. There are people that think that healing is a hoax. God can heal you from sickness and disease as well as from emotional scars and broken relationships. Be bold today and share your authentic testimony with someone else that they too can get connected or reconnected with God, so that in time they too will soon have *Bold & Crazy Faith*!

CHAPTER 9 -BOLDNESS IN YOUR WITNESS
BOLD OBSERVATIONS

_____

_____

_____

_____

_____

_____

_____

_____

_____

_____

_____

_____

_____

_____

CHAPTER 9 -BOLDNESS IN YOUR WITNESS
BOLD OBSERVATIONS

_____

_____

_____

_____

_____

_____

_____

_____

_____

_____

_____

_____

_____

_____

CHAPTER 9 -BOLDNESS IN YOUR WITNESS
BOLD OBSERVATIONS

_____

_____

_____

_____

_____

_____

_____

_____

_____

_____

_____

_____

_____

_____

CHAPTER 9 -BOLDNESS IN YOUR WITNESS
BOLD OBSERVATIONS

_____

_____

_____

_____

_____

_____

_____

_____

_____

_____

_____

_____

_____

CHAPTER 9 -BOLDNESS IN YOUR WITNESS
BOLD OBSERVATIONS

CHAPTER 9 -BOLDNESS IN YOUR WITNESS
FINAL OBSERVATIONS & ACTIONS

_____

_____

_____

_____

_____

_____

_____

_____

_____

_____

_____

_____

_____

_____

_____

CHAPTER 10

Boldness in God's Silence

"It's one thing to be in the middle of a trial that has been brought on by yourself through a bad choice or action. But it's an entirely different thing to set your heart on serving God only to discover that it seems He has abandoned you in the middle of a storm. In times like those, remember that although God may be silent, He is not still. Wait on Him. He may just come walking to you on top of your storm."

— **Tony Evans**

INSPIRATION

One of the things that you will encounter as a Christian is God's silence. Sometimes God is silent. However, at other times, God only *appears* to be silent. So you might ask, what do you do when it appears that God is silent? The answer is you listen. You listen to hear from God. When you listen, you may realize that God really is not silent. It's just that you are not listening to Him. You may not be hearing Him for any number of reasons. It may just be your key focus is working extra hours be cause of a financial want or need to increase your income. Maybe you are overwhelmed with school and have put your devotional time with God on the backburner. Or, just maybe it is a project that you are working on that has distracted you from your normal routine of having a devotional time with God. Maybe your attendance at church has decreased, thus eliminating your main source of hearing God through your pastor's sermon, bible study or songs from the choir.

God wants us to be obedient and as my pastor teaches us that "being obedient is fully listening to God."

There are times when God is silent. To know God is knowing He is intentional when He does things. He always does things with the objective of fulfilling His purposes. In other words, He's not being silent for no reason. His purposes are vast, so, you should recognize whatever God is doing, it is for your good. Scripture reminds us of this. According to Romans 8:28, all things work together for the good of those who love him, who have been called according to his purpose (NIV). Again, know that in His silence. God is always working. He is always working on your behalf. Like gospel recording artist William Murphy says in his gospel powerhouse album entitled, "Working", "*He's leaning in my direction.*" God is growing and strengthening you in these times. When you experience God's silence, PRAY.

Eternal God, I exalt you. You are awesome, mighty, powerful and loving.
You are the King of Kings and you are in control.
I confess that I have not put you first and need to reprioritize my life.
Thank you for being in my life.
Even when I do not hear you, I know that you are always there.

You say in your word that you will never leave me
nor forsake me.
Eternal God, I am listening, and you have my
undivided attention.
Direct my path.
In the name of Jesus, I pray, amen.

God is teaching you in these silent times to listen fully to what He is directing you to do. Listen intently to what He is saying to you. This means you should intentionally seek His direction, instruction and guidance. God wants your undivided attention. He realizes that you have a ton on your plate. He knows the things that you will encounter before you do. While He does not want all your time, He wants to be your priority. Yes, even before your family. Some people don't understand that, but because of who He is, God commands us to put Him first. The bible declares, "But seek first his kingdom and his righteousness, and all these things will be given to you as well (Matthew 6:33, NIV). The bible goes on to say, "I love them that love me; and those that seek me early shall find me (Proverbs 8:17, KJV).

If you are concerned that God is silent, maybe He wants you to come to Him. The bible says, "You will seek me and find me when you seek me with all your heart (Jeremiah 29:13, NIV). Maybe He wants you to search and examine your life and your priorities as well as any neglect of Him. After all, He is the one who can keep you from falling and also the one who blessed you exceedingly and abundantly.

Further, He is the one who provided the power as the Holy Spirit came upon you. He is the one who was with you when you witnessed and testified about His goodness to your friends and people that you encountered on vacation. He gave you the right things to say. God let you know, you were being highly effective in your witness. Those were times when chill bumps ran up and down your arms while you talked about His goodness. He was the one that got you out of the bar and off of the street. He was the one that orchestrated that promotion when you knew that you could not last one more day on that dead-end job. God was the one that convicted you through His spirit to stop being promiscuous. He was the one that orchestrated and handpicked that beautiful wife for you. Yes, the wife that lined up with His word. The bible declares, "He who finds a wife finds what is good and receives favor from the LORD (Proverbs 18:22, NIV)." God was the one that heard your prayers when your son or daughter was rebellious and did not listen to anything that you had to say. Now those same children are asking to go to church and sing on the choir. Yes, He wants your attention first and foremost.

Sometimes God uses His silence to test you. This is his way of getting your attention. Will you praise Him when He's silent? He knows whether you will or not, but do you? God wants to know if you will speak boldly about his goodness when it feels like He has left you. Will you magnify Him when it appears that He is not moving in your life? God wants to know that you will still be bold in your faith when illness strikes your body and you are in a hospital bed trying to figure out what is going on. It is through these tests that your resolve is strengthened. God tests and stretches your faith so that He can develop and mature you even in adversity. In doing so, you learn to still be bold when God is silent. No matter what, just remember that "The LORD your God is with you, the Mighty Warrior who saves. He will take great delight in you; in his love he will no longer rebuke you but will rejoice over you with singing (Zephaniah 3:17, NIV).

LIFE EXPERIENCE

As time goes on and you continue to grow spiritually, it becomes easier to deal with life when God is silent. With growth and maturity, you understand that God is always there even though you may not know what the silence means. You may begin to examine your life and ask yourself questions and ask God questions to understand where the silence is coming from. For example, you may want to ask in what area of your life is God directing the silence? You may say, "Why now, God?" Or, you may say, "Did I do something wrong that you need me to acknowledge, recognize, repent or fix? Or, you may say, "God I know you are working something out and whatever it is, I know it's for my good'. During this time, you can exalt God, praise Him and thank God in advance for helping you. Even if it is painful you can say, Lord, if it comes from you, I know it is just. You will know that ultimately the silence is for your good. Giving Him your obedience, praise and thanksgiving is the course of action that you should be taking when God is silent because it exemplifies your trust and belief that God is working for your good.

I once had a job as a sales representative with a very well-known security company in New Jersey. During the interview with the supervisor, I not only shared my past sales experience, but I also revealed my sales reports with the details of my sales rankings nationally, regionally, state-wise and even within my prior office. Most of what I shared verbally I was able to back it up with sales figures representing my work and worth. Based on my outstanding sales experience and background, I was hired to work in a division of the company that catered to affluent homeowners. The homes were much larger than the average home in the area, which meant larger sales that converted into more commission and money for me. I was ecstatic and anxious to begin.

From the very beginning, I excelled. Everything was working as expected on my end. I was more than confident in my abilities. Essentially, I just continued where I left off at the company that I quit prior to coming on board in my new position with the security company. I used the structure of making a sales presentation that the security company taught us in training. However, when it came to raw sales skills, communication and follow up, I used the same skills and methods that I did in my prior experience that usually paid huge dividends. From the outset, I had bold confidence based on my abilities, experience, and prior success, and, let's not forget, most importantly, favorable standing with God. Boldness comes mostly from knowing that you have favor. God is faithful and He is good! I knew that I had God's favor. I fully expected to do well right off the bat because I had *Bold & Crazy Faith*! But there is more.

After about four or five months, I noticed a change. The leads that I had been getting had decreased drastically. Instead of getting one or two company leads a day, I was now getting one or two company leads a week. That was a tough pill to swallow because my opportunity to convert good sales leads into actual sales had dwindled in half. I could not understand why my sales leads had almost stopped altogether until I realized the top sales representative that had been out on sick leave returned and was getting most of the leads. Subsequently, another sales representative who started about three months after I did began receiving more leads than I had as well. Concerned, I asked to meet with my supervisor with the hopes of addressing the decrease in my leads. The meeting was not very productive, and the supervisor never provided any legitimate reason for my decrease in leads. His explanation was that my territory was not producing as many leads. In reality, the other sales representatives were getting my leads. That was the truth. Never in any form was I cocky or arrogant in my dealings with my supervisor or my co-workers. It is not my personality to act as such.

However, because of the *Bold & Crazy Faith* that I obtained over the years as a result of having favor with the Lord Jesus Christ, my sales figures before the decrease were excellent. My sales figures lined up with the performance that I believed I was capable of which I also shared with my supervisor during my interview. In retrospect, I really don't think that he believed that I would start off as fast as I did. Even with the proof that I provided, I really don't think he believed it would happen that quickly. To be honest, I don't think that he ever met anyone who had the *Bold & Crazy Faith* that I did. He may have never met someone who truly believes and knows that you will receive power when the Holy Spirit has come upon you! And that is the same power that you have, too, through Him.

So, I prayed continuously on the leads and the salesman situation. It was weird because it appeared that God was silent. I had been doing very well and then suddenly everything dried up. It felt like the rug had been pulled from underneath me. The unusual thing then was that when I prayed, there was silence. When I thought about the situation, there was silence. However, in it all, I had peace. I wasn't making the money that I had been, but I had peace. There were bills that had to be paid but there was peace. During our one-on-one weekly meetings, my supervisor would say things that would have usually gotten under my skin. I had a peace that everything was going to work out in the end, even though I was being treated unfairly. Do you ever feel like someone is trying to bait you into saying something or doing something that you will regret or get you into big trouble?

This was the situation that I was in. I often thought that this supervisor was probably saying to himself,

"How can this guy be this calm after I just said that? Or, how come he is still sticking around? He is surely not buying any

thing that I am telling him about the change in leads and his performance. He has pretty much shared that with me in so many words, in a very nice manner, even knowing how rotten I have been to him.

After another month or two passed, I tried to reason eloquently with my supervisor in weekly meetings about the number of leads that he promised but I was not receiving. During that time, I also started trying to survive almost totally on creative salesmanship in getting my own appointments, leads, and referrals. I knew after six months of needing to do all that, the writing was on the wall. I knew that my days were numbered because no matter how good you claim to be, you can't make a great living in that industry without company leads. Believe it or not, I managed to make it another six months. Barely!

However unconventional, after six months I intentionally made a decision to stay at least one year. At that point I figured that it would be best to complete at least one year to keep a good record as far my work history, time on the job, etc. It was hard. But the Lord did provide. The Lord kept making ways out of no way just as He always had. Every time my back was up against the wall, a different kind of miracle happened. I would get a referral, or a person would call me out of nowhere saying they were interested in our service and would want me to come to their home or business to present. Every unexpected call resulted in a sale. People would return my calls from months prior after I had long forgotten that I even made the original call to follow up. And get this, these returned calls were from me just offering to come out and give them a free evaluation. BUT GOD! It would result in a sale like clockwork.

God will always make sure that you have enough. And truly that is all that we really need. But when God knows that we want a little something extra to get by or need a reward to help us emotionally, He is right there for that, too. And at times He will pour out blessings that you do not have enough room for. By the time I left, my company leads had decreased to only one a week which equates to four or maybe five a month. Kapoof! My well had run dry, but someone else's well was overflowing. Not fair is an understatement. Yet, I still had peace. God was providing peace in the middle of what was supposed to be a storm. I knew that it was only a matter of time before my breakthrough presented itself. One year later, I accepted an offer to be a supervisor at one of the leading retail companies in the country. God is MAGNIFICENT!

The commission sales business can be brutal. Right before starting my job with the security company, I worked as an outside sales representative at a well-known pest control company that was the leader in its industry. At that time, God had been showing me crazy almost unbelievable things that He could do. And more importantly He was showing me unbelievable things that He could do with me. Here I am reminded of a song "Over and Over" by Trinity 5:7, that is so applicable to that time in my life. The theme of the song is, God will bless you over and over again, even when you are not   deserving. God kept blessing me beyond my wildest expectations. I knew that God was capable of doing all things, but when supernatural things happen to you, it takes on a whole new meaning.

I mentioned earlier in chapter seven, we sometimes put a limit on God as to how much we think He is capable of doing. At other times you limit what you think He will do for you. You cannot think when God does something for you, He automatically must move on to the next person because your turn is over and it's someone else's turn now. No. He can bless the next person at the same time He is still blessing you! Yes, He can. God doesn't have a box or a lane that stops Him from thinking about you while He is thinking about me at the same time. He is God and He is sovereign. He can do anything at any time He wants. Do you remember the song, "He's Got the Whole World in His Hand?" This is the King of kings and the Lord of lords that we are talking about. We are not talking about UncleEddie or Aunt Geneva who may or may not show up if you need a ride from the bowling alley. God is able! Yes, He is.

There have been times in my past work experiences that God did things that could not be humanly possible. I once got suspended at the pest control company for two days. My boss reprimanded me for not setting the minimum amount of daily appointments required to meet the standards set for our branch. The procedure for making appointments was to make calls to existing customers and offer a free inspection as a way of checking to see if they were having any issues. The main objective however was to sell an additional service that the company offered.

Setting the standard quantity of appointments was very important to the success of the company but doing so was very challenging. Most of the time because of time constraints the sales representatives would fall short by one or two appointments a day.

Many of us took a phone list with us to call during the day while we were driving to appointments. The hope was to set the one or two appointments that you could not set on call night or during morning appointment-setting after the sales meeting. The company knew by setting a very high standard of seven appointments daily, sales representatives would consistently set four or five appointments which was enough to walk away with a sale or two. Even though I rarely met the standard for setting appointments like the rest of my colleagues, I usually did well at converting calls into appointments. After working there for so many years, I homed in on my gifts of verbal communications and creativity to set appointments and close sales at a high percentage. But, on this day, my boss chose to make me an example. I say this with sincerity because everyone knew the standard of setting seven appointments every day was unrealistic.

Upon my arrival back to the office, my boss asked to speak to me in her office. She gave me a two-day suspension for not meeting the company standard for appointments. My response was that I sometimes met the standard for appointments and sometimes I didn't, just like all the other sales representatives. I mentioned that I usually did better setting appointments than most of the other sales representatives and my sales reflected that. I told her that she was not being fair. Everyone knew there were too many variables that came into play when making appointments to consistently hit the standard. Some of the variables included: The amount of time it took completing supporting documentation at the office that accompanied the contracts from the days sales. If you had two or three sales, it would take a long time before you could begin making your calls to set appointments. Did the service manager want to discuss details on your graphs to properly treat the homes? How about needing to call one of your customers who canceled to save the sale? Here is my favorite. The husband or wife that calls you while you are setting appointments, to discuss all the details of your findings and presentation that you shared with their spouse earlier in the day. As you can see, appointment setting was very challenging for many reasons.

So, she suspended me. To add insult to injury, she said, "while you are home for the next two days, think about how important this job is to you". I couldn't believe it. I had just established myself as one of the top sales representatives in the state and region. She told me to come back in two days and report to work at 8:00am to meet again in her office. I went home and shared the news with my wife like I always do when something important happens.

As requested, I reported to work two days later and met with her again inside her office. After our meeting she told me to go into the sales office, set only five appointments because of the time, and run my appointments for the day. Pretty ironic to approve five appointments on this day when time had always been the deciding factor as to the amount of qualified appointments you could realistically and consistently set daily.

When I walked into the sales office, the other sales representative had already gone to start their day. So, there I was, alone making calls in an empty office that was exceptionally quiet. Angry because I didn't make any money for the two days I was suspended and because I felt disrespected and taken advantage of. I knew that my boss was making an example to the rest of the office, but I found out later from one of my colleagues that the sales manager was told that if they intentionally got under my skin, it would make me sell better. Do you believe that?!

I arrived at my first appointment that day at approximately 12:45 pm, quite a few hours from my normal time of arrival to a first appointment. That means I would leave the office at approximately 7:15 – 7:30 am. I liked to get out early. As you may have noticed, this was a very late start for me. At 12:45 pm, I would usually be finishing my third appointment and heading to my fourth. I didn't mention earlier that it was February in New Jersey, and the temperature was in the twenties. The time of the year is key to explaining the supernatural power and favor that I experienced with God as I worked in the pest control industry because people are reluctant to buy new contracts during the winter months. They somehow think they are immune from bug infestation.

In February they had sales representatives that would sometimes go two weeks straight without a sale. Do the math. That is five appointments a day because no one ever really got seven appointments except for during swarm season. During swarm season, the phones would ring off the hook because homeowners would be alarmed from termites swarming inside their homes. The leads were plentiful, and the money was great during this time of the year. In the winter months, things would look quite differently. Five appointments a day, six days a week because we worked on Saturdays. That is 30 appointments a week and 60 appointments in 2 weeks with 0 sales. That is 0 sales in 60 appointments.

This was February! As I began my day, one appointment after the next, I would find live termites during each inspection. One appointment after the next I would sell the company's termite service to a homeowner. As I continued my day, one appointment after the next the homeowner would be home anticipating my arrival like they said they would. On average, there would be at least one cancellation. But not on this twenty something degree day in February on the Jersey Shore. No, no. Not on this day.

Later in the day as I continued, I did not find issues inside or outside the homes but consulted the homeowners professionally and respectfully, convincing them to protect their homes which were usually their greatest investment. On this day the Lord showed up in a mighty way. Redemption is mine says, the Lord! At the end of the day I sold five termite contracts for $7,500 in total sales. At a 17 to 20 0% commission, I made between $1,300 and $1,500 in one day. In February, the dead of winter! That was good money approximately 15 to 20 years ago as it is today. Did I make my money back from being suspended for two days? Absolutely, and then some! There were sales representatives that did not make that in the entire month of February. I had five sales in five appointments (5 for 5). I closed 100% of my appointments on a twenty-something-degree day in February. Now you tell me that God isn't good.

God blew my mind on this job. I have many other stories like this one that goes beyond human logic. No way, no how did I do this. It was all God. Remember, the other sales representatives left the office long before I started making appointments. They didn't even see me that morning. I knew that when they came into the office and looked at the sales board inside the office branch, they would be flabbergasted. When I walked into the branch, I couldn't believe what I saw on the sales board. Do you know that none of the other sales representatives had a sale from the previous day? We had about twelve or thirteen sales representatives and nobody had a sale next to their name but me. I had five sales next to my name from the previous day. Five sales in twenty something degree weather in February for $7,500. All the sales were termite contracts which were the hardest ones to come by because they were so expensive. I walked through the doors looked up and said, What! I couldn't believe it. Surprised as I was about getting suspended, I was more surprised no one else got a sale for the entire day. I worked there for almost seven years and I never saw only one person make a sale in a full day.

Of course, some of the sales representatives wanted to know how I was able to have that kind of day. Do you know what my answer was? God! Plain and simple. Nothing but God! My boss tried to attribute my phenomenal day to having good appointments. Really? Are you serious? So, it was the boss's suspension that forced me to get good appointments which in turn accounted for five termite contracts in right, you guessed it, twenty something degree weather in February. If that was true, she should have suspended the other 11 or 12 sales representatives that chucked zeroes so they could have also had five sales in twenty something degree weather in February.

What the boss did not understand was where she thought getting me angry was bringing forth the huge results that the branch desired. This was not the case at all. God was redeeming, protecting, developing and inspiring me to move towards where I am right now in my life and beyond. The boss and my peers knew that it was something different about me which they could not put into terms. My boss on occasion would call me Reverend Ramsey even before I got ordained as a Deacon. You see, even though it was very hard, I did my best and had my own way of representing God in a toxic environment. They used me to train new sales representatives in the field. So many of the new employees expressed what I was doing was amazing. Many of them asked how I managed to sell so well. My answer was always the same. God! I'm blessed. God set me up in situations and scenarios that only He could create that were ideal for miracles.

Some of the new employees would be amazed when we got into the homes as they saw me engage and interact with homeowners. A few new employees even told me they initially thought I was lying to people until they watched and talked to me while I trained them. I asked them to explain what they meant. Their response was how else can you put up big sales numbers like you do and be consistent. My response was that I am a gifted salesman however, I have the favor of God on my life which is the most important thing.

With some, I would sit in my car with them for a few hours explaining how to sell and some of my past experiences with customers. On many occasions I would get the chills as I explained passionately about being creative with different ways to get sales beyond the textbook company presentation that was tried and true. God will do exceedingly abundantly beyond all we ask or think (Ephesians 3:20, NIV). And to think that God is still doing mind-boggling things today in my life some 15 to 20 years later. Writing this book is another one of those things that I would never have imagined during this time in my life. Never! If you just read this and you don't know God for yourself, I think now is a great time to make the decision to give your life to Him. A God who performs supernatural things such as these and has that kind of power is good to have in your life.

Eventually, within the company, I would be rated as one of the Top 100 sales representatives in the country. I learned more about the awesome limitless power of God in the six to seven years that I spent as an outside sales representative with the pest control company than I ever have in my life. But even with all the blessings that God was giving me, the business processes, pay plan and the people had changed drastically since I started. God had been telling me to leave for years even before the changes took place.

I finally made an exit after things had gotten so bad. The respect that I have for myself had been tested one too many times and I had had enough. Things got so bad that I quit without having another job. My mother passed away after a sudden illness during this time, and it really made me take a hard look at everything that was going on in my life. Among the changes that I mentioned above, my job was very unsympathetic during the one month of my mother's illness and subsequent passing. Ultimately, this was the last straw and final factor in my decision to quit. In less than a week I found another job and received an offer from the security company! God is faithful! My loving wife Deb had known for years everything that I had been dealing with on this job and supported me in my decision. I am very thankful to have a wife that supports me. With that in mind, I was confident enough to step out on faith and quit without having a job. I would not usually advise anyone quit a job without having another one. However, if God is telling you to leave—*leave*! If you know that God has something else for you, go! I promised myself that I would never again not listen to God. He had been trying to push me out for years, but I just didn't listen. The money was good at the time and I remember pleading with God saying, "Lord, I know that you want me to leave, but this is the busy time of the year. After I make my money during this time, I will find another job." But God's plans are the right plans, and He knows how to push you along the way even if you are kicking and screaming while He is doing it. God knows best.

BIBLICAL EXAMPLE

In the gospels, there is a story of a Canaanite woman who approached Jesus asking for mercy. In faith, she begged for healing for her demon-possessed daughter. Initially, Jesus did not answer the woman. His disciples pleaded to Jesus to send her away because she kept shouting at them. Breaking His silence, Jesus said that He was only sent to the lost sheep of Israel.

The woman came and bowed before Him.

"Lord, help me!"

Jesus said, "It is not good to throw the children's bread to the dogs".

The Canaanite woman responded. "Yes Lord; but even dogs feed on crumbs that fall from their master's table."

"Woman, your faith is great" Jesus replied. "It will be done for you as you wish."

The woman's daughter was healed immediately.

Even in God's silence, make your request continually and wait for God's answer. Be patient, keep a great attitude and trust the His process.

BOLD CONCLUSION

Maturity in your walk is recognizing that maybe God is waiting for you to act and wants you to step up to the plate and use the gifts that He has given you. God will test you in various ways and silence is one of them. What will you do? How will you react when you have gotten used to hearing from God? Will you be like a child who learns how to ride a bicycle using training wheels at the beginning, then eventually graduate to one training wheel?

Similarly, there comes a time for you to sink or swim. God will never let you sink completely. As a Father, He will do what He needs to get you to where He wants you to be. You should be one of God's biggest cheerleaders as a full-fledged representative for the body of Christ. As such, you can even explain to others how you trust God even when He is silent.

CHAPTER 10 -BOLDNESS IN GODS SILENCE
BOLD OBSERVATIONS

CHAPTER 10 -BOLDNESS IN GODS SILENCE
BOLD OBSERVATIONS

CHAPTER 10 -BOLDNESS IN GODS SILENCE
BOLD OBSERVATIONS

_____

_____

_____

_____

_____

_____

_____

_____

_____

_____

_____

_____

_____

_____

CHAPTER 10 -BOLDNESS IN GODS SILENCE
BOLD OBSERVATIONS

_____

_____

_____

_____

_____

_____

_____

_____

_____

_____

_____

_____

_____

CHAPTER 10 -BOLDNESS IN GODS SILENCE
BOLD OBSERVATIONS

_____

_____

_____

_____

_____

_____

_____

_____

_____

_____

_____

_____

_____

_____

CHAPTER 10 -BOLDNESS IN GODS SILENCE
FINAL OBSERVATIONS & ACTIONS

_____

_____

_____

_____

_____

_____

_____

_____

_____

_____

_____

_____

_____

CHAPTER 11

Boldness in Prayer

*"In my deepest, darkest moments, what really got me through
was a prayer. Sometimes my prayer was 'Help me.' Sometimes a
prayer was 'Thank you.' What I've discovered is that intimate
connection and communication with my creator will always get
me through because I know my support, my help, is just a prayer
away."*

— **Iyanla Vanzant**

INSPIRATION

God wants you to be confident in your prayers. The confidence that you have in your prayers should reflect the *Bold & Crazy Faith* that you activate daily. For all intents and purposes, the boldness that you have really comes down to the level of faith and trust that you believe that God can do what He says He will do.

First, you need to believe. Not just believe that God exists but that there is no limit to what He can do. He can do anything and everything that you can imagine. You should not limit your faith in the small things. God wants us to think big because He is big. As His representative, you think like He thinks. You have heard the cliché the apple does not fall far from the tree. It is true; it does not. You are a son or daughter of God and your Father wants you to be like him. "For those God foreknew, he also predestined to be conformed to the image of his Son, that he might be the first-born among many brothers and sisters" (Romans 8:29, NIV).

Naturally you are not God. However, you are one of His descendants and the bible teaches that we are to follow His model. God is omnipotent which means he is all-powerful, over all things always. He is also omnipresent which means God is everywhere at the same time.

Next, you need to trust God for who He is. To trust God is to be bold for God. If you trust Him, your life would reflect your trust. Do you trust that He will be with you even until the end of the world? Do you believe that God is a healer? Do you believe that He will pour out a blessing that you don't have room to re-ceive? When you do trust, you will have joy and peace. And when you trust, you will have a *Bold & Crazy Faith* that may even sur-prise you.

Additionally, you should draw from your life experiences and successes in prayer. Your life experiences are a testament to what God has already done in your life. God honors acknowledge-ment of the things that He has done for you. You will also receive a boldness that goes along with knowing that God was able and de-livered. Your boldness in prayer will increase overtime with your continual victories in your life. The boldness that you have in prayer is also effective when praying for others. The confidence that you exude will be felt by them and will help to increase their faith in return.

LIFE EXPERIENCE

In your lifetime you will have plenty of opportunities to pray. There will even be times when you will be asked to pray (intercede) for others. That is, occasionally you may be led by the Holy Spirit to intercede on someone's behalf. Even now as I am writing, God has placed someone in my spirit that I will see tomorrow. I know that I need to pray with that person. I already prayed for this individual privately; however, I have not prayed with that person one-on-one. I know that God has been leading me to intercede and pray with them the last few weeks, but I haven't out of the uncertainty of embarrassment on their part because our meeting is in a public place (a barber shop). Yet, God wants me to. I feel it in my spirit. I will be obedient to God and be bold in my intercession tomorrow. This does not happen to me often. You may pray (a prayer of petition) for and, at times simply pray (a prayer for blessing) for God's power and protection over a person, place or event. Other times we pray (a prayer of thanksgiving) to thank God for all the blessings that He has given us and a prayer (a prayer of praise) to give God glory because He is God.

There are many types of prayer. The point is that you should pray boldly in any prayer that you pray. How would you feel if someone prayed for you and they didn't feel confident in what they were asking God for or didn't sound like they really believed that God was hearing them? Or better yet, what if the person praying said, "God I don't know if you are up there, or if you can really hear me right now. I sure hope that you do. How about God if you really exist, help this man or woman. I just figured I'd give it a shot just in case you really exist". No way, my brother, and no way, my sister.

You need to come boldly before the throne of grace. Instead pray:

No weapon formed against this woman or man will prosper in the name of Jesus. At the name of Jesus, every knee shall bow, and EVERY tongue will confess that JESUS IS LORD! My God is the God that is faithful, a promise-keeping God. And what He promises, He is also ABLE to perform! He IS able. Yes, He IS ABLE!

God wants you to be bold in your prayers in terms of the things that you ask for. Go to the Word. Use it to pray about the things that God says He will do. Draw from His promises. Pray about the things that He has already done. Pray about the things that He has done in the bible. Remind him that in his word it says, "for where two or three are gathered together in My name, I am there in the midst of them (Matthew 18:20 NKJV)."

As you think about what you want to pray, you may come up with something like this:

You said it Lord, so I believe it and because I believe it, I know you are here and because you are here, I know that you are listening so hear me O' God. Hear my cry, here my bold request today in the name of Jesus. I remember when you made all my enemies fall by the wayside. One by one. Just as you said in your Word. They scattered and they fell. You really did make my enemies my footstools. You have shown me in the past and you continually show me time after time again. Lord, your words are life. I know you to be a promise keeper. I know you to be a burden bearer. There is nothing that you cannot fix and there is no problem that you cannot solve.

Pray boldly while asking God to: Heal and Deliver in the name of Jesus.

I acknowledge you as the King of Kings and Lord of Lords. You are worthy to be exalted. I know that you can heal anything in the manner of sickness and disease. Deliver Him Lord because you are a deliverer. Deliver Him just as you delivered the Israelites out of Egypt. You were able to part the Red Sea God so surely taking the taste of marijuana out of his mouth is a small feat for you. You have done this many times God. Take the taste away God, oh yes take it away. There is HEALING in the name of Jesus, DELIVERANCE in the name of Jesus. God your word says that No weapon formed against me will prosper. I am the head and not the tail. I know that you want me to be bold, so I am asking boldly by faith that you will heal, deliver and provide peace according to your word. So, I am calling those things that are not as though they are, the bible says, old things have passed, behold all things have become new. Thank you God. In the name of Jesus, amen.

As a simple guide, use the **ACTS** prayer format to pray boldly in prayer.

Acknowledgement (Acknowledge God for who He is)
Confession (Confess your sins and ask forgiveness)
Thanksgiving (Thank God for His blessings)
Supplication (Ask God or Make Request).

Then, end your prayers in the **name of Jesus**.

BIBLICAL EXAMPLE

Jesus used the Lord's Prayer to teach the disciples how to pray with boldness and persistence. Use Luke 11:1-13 from The Message (MSG) to meditate on what you are asking.

BOLD CONCLUSION

When things are down, know that you can call on God. The old folks used to say He may not come when you need Him, but He is always right on time. Have you experienced this? If you have, then let somebody know about it. Trust God and have the bold confidence that He will answer your prayers.

The bible declares that "blessed is the one who trusts in the LORD, whose confidence is in him. [8]They will be like a tree planted by the water that sends out its roots by the stream. It does not fear when heat comes; its leaves are always green. It has no worries in a year of drought and never fails to bear fruit (Jeremiah 17:7,8, NIV). With that said, be blessed, my brother and sister. Be bold in your prayers and trust God in every area of your life. He will intercede on your behalf. Be bold and trust God when you pray about your finances. Trust God when you pray about your marriage. Trust that God will answer your prayers and send the right mate for you in due season. Exude your boldness and trust God for favorable results when you are praying for your health and the health of others.

There is no limit to what God can do. Therefore, your knowledge of this should be exercised in your prayer life. Even during your prayer, God can give you the knowledge of topics to pray about. Oh yes, He is amazing. God is all of that and then some. He is greater than the riches of riches. He is more important than wealth. God is even more important than your health. Do you believe that? Do you know Him for yourself? Trust God to be bold in your prayers! Don't wait until He does something good for you to be bold in your prayers. Be bold that God will answer your prayers even when the chips are down. Over time, your faith will increase steadily through experiences and positive results. You have every reason to be bold in prayer and be blessed to live an abundant life in Christ.

CHAPTER 11 -BOLDNESS IN PRAYER
BOLD OBSERVATIONS

CHAPTER 11 -BOLDNESS IN PRAYER
BOLD OBSERVATIONS

_____

_____

_____

_____

_____

_____

_____

_____

_____

_____

_____

_____

_____

_____

_____

CHAPTER 11 -BOLDNESS IN PRAYER
BOLD OBSERVATIONS

CHAPTER 11 -BOLDNESS IN PRAYER
BOLD OBSERVATIONS

_____

_____

_____

_____

_____

_____

_____

_____

_____

_____

_____

_____

_____

_____

_____

_____

CHAPTER 11 -BOLDNESS IN PRAYER
BOLD OBSERVATIONS

CHAPTER 11 -BOLDNESS IN PRAYER
FINAL OBSERVATIONS & ACTIONS

_____

_____

_____

_____

_____

_____

_____

_____

_____

_____

_____

_____

_____

_____

_____

_____

CHAPTER 12

Negative Influences and Associations

"Never allow people who aren't going anywhere to take you with them."

— **Myles Monroe**

INSPIRATION

The Christian lifestyle is a very rewarding alternative to the way that the world chooses to live. Yet, with all the rewards, there are challenges that come with the territory of being a Christian. One of the biggest challenges you face as a born-again Christian comes by way of negative influences and associations.

Negative influences and associations come in many forms. They can be described as things that are not good for you. They hinder you from being the best that you can be. Negative influences and associations can distract you and infringe on your space or privacy. Simply put, they will stunt your spiritual growth. They discourage you from proceeding with God's plan for your life.

Let's take a closer look at a few examples of negative influences. Alcohol and drug abuse is obviously a negative influence. If you are abusing alcohol and drugs, your state of mind is being altered on a regular basis; therefore, you cannot focus on God. Anything addictive in nature, including sexual promiscuity, that has you bound and away from the will that God has for your life is a negative influence. Negative influences take you off course. They keep you from being productive executing the plans that God has for you in your Christian journey.

Anything that stops you from pleasing God can be considered a negative influence. Negative influences affect your faith. You CAN NOT be BOLD in the things of God if you are being negatively influenced. Yes, it is true that we all fall short, but you do not want to keep falling short again and again to become a built-in excuse for sinning. The more you fall short and accept it, without feeling bad about the sin, it becomes easier the next time to submit to the negative influences that are around you. Before long, you may give up on striving for the excellence that God is calling you to.

Negative associations can be described as individuals or groups of people that are not good for you for many reasons. Everyone will not be happy for you when you live for Christ to include   acquaintances, friends, family and co-workers. There is a cliché in the African-American church that states, "more levels, more devils." The meaning is centered on the belief that the devil intensifies attacks, the closer your relationship becomes with God. Satan is a tireless foe who sometimes works through people to get you off your game. Satan will indeed throw everything at you including the kitchen sink. So be ready at all times for the persecution. Better yet, *expect and prepare* for the persecution. Jesus was persecuted and you will be as well.

During your faith walk, there is no easier way to sabotage your life and effectiveness than harboring negative influences and associations in your life. To maximize the return on the investment that Jesus made for you on the cross, steer clear from negative influences and associations that will impact your faith and be detrimental to your Christian journey.

LIFE EXPERIENCE

As you already know, life is challenging even without the negative influences and associations with some people, places and things. Having people in your life who do not have your best interest at heart will just add fuel to the fire. To be able to accomplish the plans that God has designed for you specifically, you need to limit or sever some of your associations. It may sound harsh, but this may be the best piece of advice that I can give you. Just think of it as pruning. To prune a tree or shrub, you must remove the weeds or excess so that the tree or shrub can grow. It's no different with your life and walk with Christ. God wants you to rid yourself of excess baggage in the form of people that are weighing you down or poisoning your mind body and spirit with negative thoughts, words and actions. Negative communication will drain you and cause you to falter and not succeed in what God wants you to do.

God wants to take you to a place of prosperity. He wants to take you away from the barren land to a place where creativity, production and life are thriving all around you. Your High Priest wants to elevate you to new levels in the Kingdom, but he cannot do it until you adhere to his direction of removing people that are not beneficial to your growth and development. Some of your associations will sever ties with you anyway or limit the amount of time they spend with you because people tend to grow apart and change directions in their lives.

My pastor once commented that most of our relationships are really 'situationships'. What he means is that mostly everyone we have an association with is really a situational relationship, a relationship that is not foundational. It is just a relation on the surface built around a situation. The 'situationship' could involve coworkers where you are associated through work only. Your 'situationship' could be a teammate on your bowling team. It may be through a service with your barber, hairstylist, or car wash attendant. Your 'sitiationship' could be with your doctor or dentist. To that end, most people are not considered friends.

Most people can count their *true* friends on one hand. Indeed, if you are really being truthful, you can probably count one or two good friends that you know that have been with you and will be with you through thick and thin. They are the friends that will let you stay at their house if you are going through a really tough time like a divorce or mourning the loss of a loved one. If you have more than one or two people that you can call a true friend, consider yourself fortunate and very blessed. True friends come a dime a dozen and are very hard to find. I would go out on a limb to say that you really don't usually find true friendships. They find you. God knows just what you need and when you need it. He will put people in your life and He will take people out of your life. We just have to be obedient and listen fully to what God is telling us and directing us to do.

Cutting some ties and limiting others is downright necessary if you want to keep or improve your quality of life. If not, you will find yourself getting into things that will be detrimental and ruin the good name that you have as well as your witness for Christ.

BIBLICAL EXAMPLE

While speaking about the truth in the resurrection of the dead and more importantly the resurrection of Christ, the Apostle Paul counseled the Corinthians about both the deception and the dangers of keeping bad company. He warns "bad company corrupts good character. Come back to your senses as you ought, and stop sinning, for there are some who are ignorant of God. I say this to your shame" (1 Corinthians 15:33,34, NIV).

BOLD CONCLUSION

Negative influences and associations can and will destroy you. So, take your time in getting to know people. Be selective as to whom you spend your time with. Surround yourself with people that truly have your best interest. Use your spiritual antennae to discern when God is bringing or sending someone into your life. In doing so, you will satisfy God, identifying and gaining access to the purpose that God has for your acquaintance.

People who have your best interest want to see you reach your full potential and achieve every goal that you set out to achieve. They are not competitive with you. Instead, they are rooting for you the whole time along the way. Their positive spirit and encouragement provide energy and confidence that helps you to succeed. In short, they are your ride or die. They are genuine folks that are always in your corner no matter what. Summarily, they are considered positive influences and associations. Positive influences and associations build you up and help you get to the next level. They are not "yes" men or women; they will hold you accountable when you screw up. There is nothing like having someone in your corner who will check you because they sincerely want to see you do well. This is an example of what the bible means by iron sharpening iron (Proverbs 27:17, NIV).

If you want to have *Bold & Crazy Faith*, connect with people who are on your level. For example, people that are on your level have a better chance of understanding some things that you are going through because they may be going through or gone through the same thing themselves. Why? Because the variables and commonality in your lifestyles are more likely to bring on the same encounters and challenges. They can help you navigate through the processes to gain favorable outcomes. Therefore, if you want to have *Bold & Crazy Faith*, link up with positive people that you can learn from and add value to your life. Link up with folks that can show you things that you have never experienced. These positive associations will encourage you and boost your confidence through positive support, reinforcement and accountability to succeed. This is a source of your boldness. As I stipulated before, many of these folks have already gone through some of the things that you are going through and can be a great help to you.

Watch and identify those that seem to fade out of your life the more you begin to accomplish your goals and dreams. As you accomplish one goal after the next, you will begin to see people slipping away from you. The sad truth is some people hate to see others succeed, even those they claim as friends. They hate it. Although it will sometimes be hard, let them slip away and don't worry about HATERATION! Use HATERAID as motivation to catapult you to higher heights and propel you into the destiny that God has for your life. This much is true: this will happen when you begin to dream big and see those big dreams come to pass.

As you step out on faith, the more you achieve at your goals, the bolder you will become. So, be bold, my brother. Be bold, my sister in the things of God. Always do your best in representing Our Lord and Savior Jesus The Christ, for he is a STRONG TOWER and our help. Remember, the power you need for everything comes from Him.

CHAPTER 12 -NEGATIVE INFLUENCES & ASSOCIATIONS
BOLD OBSERVATIONS

CHAPTER 12 -NEGATIVE INFLUENCES & ASSOCIATIONS
BOLD OBSERVATIONS

_____

_____

_____

_____

_____

_____

_____

_____

_____

_____

_____

_____

_____

_____

CHAPTER 12 -NEGATIVE INFLUENCES & ASSOCIATIONS
BOLD OBSERVATIONS

_____

_____

_____

_____

_____

_____

_____

_____

_____

_____

_____

_____

_____

_____

CHAPTER 12 -NEGATIVE INFLUENCES & ASSOCIATIONS
BOLD OBSERVATIONS

_____

_____

_____

_____

_____

_____

_____

_____

_____

_____

_____

_____

_____

_____

_____

CHAPTER 12 -NEGATIVE INFLUENCES & ASSOCIATIONS
BOLD OBSERVATIONS

_____

_____

_____

_____

_____

_____

_____

_____

_____

_____

_____

_____

_____

CHAPTER 12 -NEGATIVE INFLUENCES & ASSOCIATIONS
FINAL OBSERVATIONS & ACTIONS

_____

_____

_____

_____

_____

_____

_____

_____

_____

_____

_____

_____

_____

_____

CHAPTER 13

Persevering In Your Christian Journey

"You will be wounded many times in your life. You'll make mistakes. Some people will call them failures, but I have learned that failure is really God's way of saying, "Excuse me, you're moving in the wrong direction." It's just an experience, just an experience."

— **Oprah Winfrey**

INSPIRATION

The Christian journey represents a cornucopia of experiences. It is filled with mountain top experiences and valley moments. As a born-again believer, I hope you have experienced the dramatic highs that come with the Christian Lifestyle and blessings of our Lord and Savior Jesus Christ. For instance, maybe you have seen the favor of God in your selection for a prestigious position that you know you were not the most qualified. You may also be blessed with abundant peace. The bible says, "And the peace of God, which transcends all understanding, will guard your hearts and your minds in Christ Jesus" (Philippians 4:7, NIV). Peace is one of the most joyous and wonderful blessings that God gives. The bible also says, "Peace I leave with you; my peace I give you. I do not give to you as the world gives. Do not let your hearts be troubled and do not be afraid" (John 14:27, NIV).

Conversely, you may have experienced the traumatic lows that go with the Christian lifestyle as well. You may have lost your job and unemployment may have wrecked your finances. A car accident may have disfigured your body and your self-esteem may be suffering. An unexpected divorce may have you on the verge of throwing in the towel. With the fear of being alone, you may even be contemplating suicide. Sickness and disease may have ravaged your body to the point that you thought you would not pull through. But God! He will intercede on your behalf!

And then there are times that are neither high nor low that may also be classified as silent times. In chapter 10, I talked about having bold faith even when you don't hear God. The silent times will require patience and maturity as you may become eager and anxious for God to do something new in your life. When it appears as though He is not, you may be disappointed. There are times that you pray, but it does not seem like God is there.

You will also have experiences that are predictable because of your faith, trust and maturity in your relationship with God. In these times, you live day to day. For the most part nothing seems to be too eventful. It's not that these times are considered bad. However, when you are living with God, you ARE bold and are EXPECTANT of the best. You grow accustomed to living the best life and recognize that it is not just material. Living the best life can be classified as having great health, peace and joy.

LIFE EXPERIENCE

There is much that can be said about luxury and convenience in this world today. And there is much to be said about misfortune and pain. In this journey, if you live long enough you will experience all of the above. Yes, you are blessed and have favor and all of that good stuff; however, the fact that you are reading this book means that you have already persevered through some rough terrain. You have endured the rigors of persecution from folks that you least expected would treat you in such a way. But usually the best of things usually take time and are not manufactured or produced quickly. Ergo, the persecution. This is part of the cost that we must pay to live and endure this Christian journey.

It seems that many of us want everything to come fast. For example, we like fast powerful cars with the brawny tires and fast service when we are at the bank or in the grocery store. We like to think that we are smart enough to make a fast dollar. Let's face it, in today's society, we want our cake when we want it and we always want it right now. Quite the microwave society we are. Everyone is rushing and scrambling around to see how much they can get done in record setting time. We hardly have quality time with our families these days, and when we do, it is only because we have learned to be intentional to do the things that we should be doing naturally. When it comes to getting things done, how about multi-tasking? Multi-tasking is the name of the game and if you don't multi-task you are generally thought of as not productive. But really, when you multi-task, are you really producing quality or are you just getting more than one thing done simultaneously?

Don't get me wrong. There is a place for speed and swiftness, and there are seasons that you will experience pain, disrespect

181

and deceit. I, too, like to be waited on quickly. When I am at the mall, for example, I want nothing less than quick service. When I'm at a restaurant, I do not like waiting to be seated. I want to find my own seat and get on with the business of ordering and eating. I don't like getting stuck in traffic. Yet in all these dislikes, I know that I need to take the good with the bad because living a quality life takes balance. The bible says, "the race is not always to the swift, Nor the battle to the strong, Nor satisfaction to the wise, Nor riches to the smart, Nor grace to the learned. Sooner or later bad luck hits us all" (Ecclesiastes 9:11, MSG). We all have to go through!

When the enemy comes in like a flood and it seems that all kinds of negativity is being directed towards you, this is the time to have *Bold & Crazy Faith*. When the fiery darts of the devil are coming your way, this is the time that you stand on God's word. This is the time that you declare, "God is doing something for my good and I trust and believe He is working it out." This is the time that you speak things into existence. For all intents and purposes, I know that right now I am being tried through the fire, but I will come out of these circumstances like pure gold. I may be going through right now but I will persevere in the name of Jesus.

By all accounts, this journey is just that, a journey. A slow walk full of surprises. What's behind door number one? Only God knows! What's behind door number two? Only God knows! Behind door number one may be joy. Behind door number two may be pain. You need to take it all in stride, the good with the bad and the ugly with the pretty. Just press on.

Blessed is the one who perseveres under trial because, having stood the test, that person will receive the crown of life that the Lord has promised to those who love him (James 1:12 NIV).

BIBLICAL EXAMPLE

The Apostle Paul's life is truly a testament of persevering boldly through the Christian journey. He describes the challenge of being hard pressed on every side and still be able to endure despite being confused and persecuted in his quest to share the good news of Jesus Christ. From studying Paul's life, I have come to conclude that when we believe, we have the faith to speak.

Paul describes the persecution that came with being a Christian. He was beaten, imprisoned, made to work hard and exposed to death on more than one occasion. The Apostle Paul had to endure being stoned, shipwrecks, bandits, and endangered almost everywhere that he went. He labored and often went without food, drink and sleep. He mentioned his concern for the churches. He also described his humility in talking about the things that showed his weaknesses. Yet, in all these things, Paul was not ashamed of the gospel of Jesus Christ. He preached and persevered boldly knowing the consequences would be persecution and even death.

BOLD CONCLUSION

Just like Paul, you will experience persecution as you walk in your Christian journey. Even so, never look at life like, 'my God, here comes another dark cloud.' Instead, look at life like here comes another dark cloud yet, I have lived to see another day. Another day that will get me one day closer to the sun shiny days that I long for. Oh yes, oh yes, there will be more sun-filled days in your Christian journey. In this, I promise, and in God, we trust.

The road will not always be easy, but in the end, just re-member that you already have the victory in Christ Jesus. There will be tests that come from God as a way of sharpening your sword for even tougher battles. These tests will contest you in the face of God promoting and elevating you to higher levels for the purpose He has for you. God is The Great Sustainer. He will maintain and keep you, providing all your needs along the way to help you carry out His plan. His plan is awesome indeed, handwritten exclusively for you. It comes complete with rewards, perks and favor that goes quite neatly with being his son or daughter. Just know that you are not only down with the one who is able to keep you from falling, but you are also forever linked to the One who is Undefeated. He is Lord of Life and Lord of All. God's plan for your life is saturated with favor and is sprinkled with the glory, splendor and riches that can be found in Him. This is the reason to celebrate and that is your reason to have *Bold & Crazy Faith*. Let's go!!!

CHAPTER 13 -PERSERVING IN YOUR CHRISTIAN JOURNEY
BOLD OBSERVATIONS

_____

_____

_____

_____

_____

_____

_____

_____

_____

_____

_____

_____

_____

_____

CHAPTER 13 -PERSERVING IN YOUR CHRISTIAN JOURNEY
BOLD OBSERVATIONS

_____

_____

_____

_____

_____

_____

_____

_____

_____

_____

_____

_____

_____

_____

_____

CHAPTER 13 -PERSERVING IN YOUR CHRISTIAN JOURNEY
BOLD OBSERVATIONS

CHAPTER 13 -PERSERVING IN YOUR CHRISTIAN JOURNEY
BOLD OBSERVATIONS

_____

_____

_____

_____

_____

_____

_____

_____

_____

_____

_____

_____

_____

_____

_____

CHAPTER 13 -PERSERVING IN YOUR
CHRISTIAN JOURNEY
BOLD OBSERVATIONS

_____

_____

_____

_____

_____

_____

_____

_____

_____

_____

_____

_____

_____

_____

_____

CHAPTER 13 -PERSERVING IN YOUR
CHRISTIAN JOURNEY
FINAL OBSERVATIONS & ACTIONS

CHAPTER 14

God's Promises

*"God never said that the journey would be easy, but He did say
that the arrival would be worthwhile."*

— **Max Lucado**

INSPIRATION

As you continue to grow in your faith, keep in mind that the core for your *Bold & Crazy Faith* lies in God's Promises. Simply put, if God said it, you need to believe it. That's right. God's promises are unquestionably the center of what you stand on and believe. In the end, With God on your side, how can you lose? So, YES! Get pumped for what God is going to do in your life!

The bible has thousands of promises from God to you. He promises victory, prosperity, health, wisdom and much more. God's promises are the essence of where your boldness and victorious living comes from. Our Heavenly Father promises that He is with you. In fact, one of his many names is Emanuel which means "God with us." Therefore, fear should never be on your agenda. Will you fall short in this area every now and then, absolutely? But understand that God does not want you to be fearful. The Word of God says, "do not fear, for I am with you; do not be dismayed, for I am your God. I will strengthen you and help you; I will uphold you with my righteous right hand" (Isaiah 41:10, NIV).

Even if you don't understand one of God's promises, believe it because it is His word. Where I grew up in Neptune, New Jersey, we sometimes used the slang "word is bond" which means that something said was the truth. Well, God's Word is the truth, and His word is His bond. Read, study and meditate on the promises of our Eternal God. Really think about them. The bible declares, "Finally, brothers and sisters, whatever is true, whatever is noble, whatever is right, whatever is pure, whatever is lovely, whatever is admirable—if anything is excellent or praiseworthy—think about such things" (Philippians 4:8, NIV). Memorize the Scriptures that minister to your spirit while reading them. Absorb them. Internalize them to the point that they begin to resonate deep within. This will be the foundation and support to the faithful actions that you will take as a result of your trust in His promises.

God is limitless and lucid in His plans. There are no ifs or buts about them. There should be no other way to think about or get around it. You either believe the promises of God or you don't. Yes, God can do what seems to be the impossible. He can do anything but fail.

God promises to deliver you when you can't see your way out. God is your refuge and strength, an ever-present help in trouble (Psalm 46:1, NIV). Our Father can and will deliver you from all kinds of trials, including addictions. In fact, God specializes in delivery from everything to include drugs, sex, food and more. If it is an addiction or habit our Father can get rid of it in an instant. He is Master of it already being done. So, if the Son sets you free, you will be free indeed (John 8:36 NIV).

LIFE EXPERIENCE

For me, one of the most important promises that God has said is that "Never will I leave you; never will I forsake you" (Hebrews 13:5, NIV). That truth alone is a bold and powerful promise for us all. As such, you should also exercise your boldness and power from this fact that Our Heavenly Father is always there with you. There is no better support system than having the Lord on your side. How powerful is it in knowing that you have the creator of the universe that made a promise to you that He will always be there for you?

Your life experiences need to reflect the knowledge, wisdom, and understanding that you fully trust and stand on God's promises. Especially, if you trust God, and know He is there to oversee your affairs. Additionally, your life experiences (i.e., the fruit of your labor in the Lord) should be evident. People should be able to detect a difference, meaning they should detect a bold confidence in which you now live your life. Friends and family should hear *Bold & Crazy Faith* in your conversations, actions and lifestyle that line up with your beliefs in God's promises. They may not know or understand, for example, the promises of God but they will notice a peculiarity in the fact that when things are not going your way, you keep a positive outlook on the situation at hand or bounce back quickly. Although you are not perfect, others should see that you choose peace over strife. They should know that you are always ready to reconcile when there are differences in opinion. This can only be done in God's strength, knowing that in the end we have the victory through Him.

Through success and failure, victory and defeat, the difference between people that gain success more and those that don't, is the people that let God be their strength and lean on His promises usually fare better. You will see success when you defer to God in your weakness. If you are stuck on a dead-end job, turn it over to God. His strength will be made perfect in your weakness. Just like the title of Gospel recording artist CeCe Winans' song, "His Strength Is Perfect." Our connection with Christ means that we no longer need to live life by ourselves and in our own strength. The bible declares, "do not fear, for I am with you; do not be dismayed, for I am your God. I will strengthen you and help you; I will uphold you with my righteous right hand" (Isaiah 41:10, NIV).

Shackles of fear, discouragement, depression and so on will begin to fall off. You will have some pep in your step. You will have a confidence that will exude, *yeah*! *I can do this.* Some people will mistake it for arrogance or cockiness. Others will take it for just what it is—*Bold & Crazy Faith.* Ultimately, they will like it. It looks good on you and they will want some of it. You are not going to please everybody, and neither should you want to. In your maturity, you will come to find that people will generally be who they are going to be and as Bishop Thomas always reminds us of the famous quote by Maya Angelou, when people show you who they are, believe them. It's called favor. It's the *Bold & Crazy Faith* of a mature Christian who is confident in the promises of God that will be carried out in their lives. It's the Christian who understands that they have the VICTORY even when it does not look like it.

God says He is I AM! And I am here to tell you that He IS. Be bold because your Father is BOLD. He comes in all shapes, sizes and forms for He is the cloud by day and pillar of fire by night. So, you too, can change into different things as well. Reinvent yourself, change careers and ty new things. The sky is really the limit when you are a follower of the God with the masterplan. It's the *Bold & Crazy Faith* of the mature Christian, the studied Christian, the life-experienced Christian who has weathered some storms. The Christian that has had the heat in the oven turned up so much that they sometimes didn't know whether they were coming or going but knew that God would come to their rescue. He knows your coming in and your going out. Praise the Lord for the Lord is good. Sing Praises unto His name for He is pleasant.

BIBLICAL EXAMPLE

Of God's grace, the Apostle Paul wrote in 2 Corinthians 12:9 that God's grace is "sufficient for you, for [His] power is made perfect in weakness" (NIV). With that said, I will boast all the more gladly about my weaknesses, so that Christ's power may rest on me. Likewise, Paul made a conscious decision to magnify his own weaknesses knowing the wholesome strength of God in his own life was real. Paul knew that it was only the strength and power of God that granted him every success he had.

BOLD CONCLUSION

Our Heavenly Father makes a powerful declaration that assures you that He has your back. For I know the plans I have for you," declares the LORD, plans to prosper you and not to harm you, plans to give you hope and a future" (Jeremiah 29:11, NIV). This is the magnificent thing about God. He does what he says He'll do.

The Lord Strong and Mighty challenges us to ask Him in prayer for what we need and desire. "Until now you have not asked for anything in my name, ask and you will receive, and your joy will be complete" (John 16:24, NIV). Isn't it AWESOME to have the assurance that OUR Heavenly Father will answer our prayers?!

But hold on. Are you ready for the GREATEST promise of them all? THE GOD of OUR SALVATION blesses and assures us with the free gift of God's salvation. Isn't it assuring and awesome to know that The EVERLASTING FATHER promises us ETERNAL LIFE?!

God's promises are signed sealed and delivered. In fact, they are as solid as rock itself. He is better than any ally that anyone has ever had. HE IS your GREATEST ASSET. He is the GREATEST PHYSICIST the world has ever seen. God is A STRONG TOWER! He is so off the charts that there are many names to describe Him, including those that are relative to the description of His glory, wonder, brilliance, power, love, ambiance, peace, joy, truth, excellence, greatness.! The list can never be exhaustive. Honestly without Him I would not be here right now nevertheless writing a book about Him. You see He saved me. He said to me, "Everything is going to be alright." I could never repay him. He has poured out blessings that I truly don't have room for. I'm telling you today, "GET TO KNOW HIM and if you already KNOW HIM get to KNOW HIM BETTER. With God's promises how can you not be *BOLD & CRAZY* in your faith when it comes to HIM!

His promises are absolutely victorious. His promises are sustaining and maintaining. They give us the boldness that we need to overcome anything that is hindering us from moving forward to fulfill the purposes that God has for our life. "Through these he has given us his very great and precious promises, so that through them you may participate in the divine nature, having escaped the corruption in the world caused by evil desires (2 Peter 1:4, NIV)."

As I mentioned earlier, the bible is filled with thousands of promises from God. Though I've touched on a few, the list is not exhaustive. I encourage you to therefore study and devote time and research to as many as you can. With so many promises to empower you, how could you not have *Bold & Crazy Faith*, especially knowing that Our Creator made those promises? God is not one who would lie. If GOD SAID it, BELIEVE IT! Why not step into those promises?! Why not walk in those BOLD promises of God?! Why not please your Father abundantly! The bible says, without faith it is impossible to please God. How pleased would your Eternal God be if you not only had faith but had *BOLD & CRAZY FAITH*?!

Now that you are armed with more knowledge and understanding, make your impression felt in the world by pleasing your father in heaven. Fulfill the purpose that God has for you with *BOLD & CRAZY FAITH*!

CHAPTER 14 -GOD'S PROMISES
BOLD OBSERVATIONS

_____

_____

_____

_____

_____

_____

_____

_____

_____

_____

_____

_____

_____

_____

CHAPTER 14 -GOD'S PROMISES
BOLD OBSERVATIONS

CHAPTER 14 -GOD'S PROMISES
BOLD OBSERVATIONS

_____

_____

_____

_____

_____

_____

_____

_____

_____

_____

_____

_____

_____

_____

CHAPTER 14 -GOD'S PROMISES
BOLD OBSERVATIONS

CHAPTER 14 -GOD'S PROMISES
BOLD OBSERVATIONS

_____

_____

_____

_____

_____

_____

_____

_____

_____

_____

_____

_____

_____

_____

CHAPTER 14 -GOD'S PROMISES
BOLD OBSERVATIONS

BOLD EXPECTATIONS

_____

_____

_____

_____

_____

_____

_____

_____

_____

_____

_____

_____

_____

BOLD EXPECTATIONS

BOLD EXPECTATIONS

_____

_____

_____

_____

_____

_____

_____

_____

_____

_____

_____

_____

_____

_____

NOTES PAGE

Chapter 3
My Jewish Learning
https://www.myjewishlearning.com/article/the-story-of-joseph/.
Retrieved from the internet October 19, 2018 8:57 pm.

Chapter 4
AZ Quotes
https://www.azquotes.com/author/11559-Tyler_Perry. Retrieved
from the internet November 29, 2018 7:55 pm.

Chapter 5
All Christian Quotes
https://www.allchristianquotes.org/quotes/Charles_Stanley/585/.
Retrieved from the internet April 11, 2019 10:32 pm.

Chapter 7
Our Daily Bread
https://odb.org/2006/08/05/run-with-horses/ Retrieved from the
internet November 29, 2018 9:01 PM

Chapter 9
Wealthy Gorilla
https://wealthygorilla.com/16-motivational-stephen-curry-quotes-
success/#ixzz5SLMs67xH. Retrieved from the internet April 11,
2019 10:54 pm.

Chapter 10
Tony Evans, The Urban Alternative
https://tonyevans.org/when-god-is-silent-he-is-not-still/. Retrieved from the internet November 29, 2018 6:17 pm.

Chapter 13
AZ Quotes
https://www.azquotes.com/author/15820-
Oprah_Winfrey/tag/perseverance. Retrieved from the internet
November 27, 2018 8:57 pm.

Chapter 14
Amazing Facts
https://www.amazingfacts.org/bible-study/gods-promises.
Retrieved from the internet April 11, 2019 11:07 pm.

Chapter 14
Today's First 15 https://www.first15.org/02/27/god-promises-his-
strength/. Retrieved from the internet November 17, 2018 at 9:30
am.

Chapter 14
What Christians Want to Know
https://www.whatchristianswanttoknow.com/the-promises-of-
god-10-powerful-bible-verses-1/#ixzz5IseU0VU6. Retrieved
from the internet November 17, 2018 at 11:45 am.

Chapter 14
What Christians Want to Know
https://www.whatchristianswanttoknow.com/the-promises-of-
god-10-powerful-bible-verses-1/#ixzz5IsdnSEnm. Retrieved
from the internet November 17, 2018 12:13 pm.

Chapter 14
20 Amazing Quotes by Max Lucado
Read more: https://www.christianquotes.info/top-quotes/20-
amazing-quotes-by-max-lucado/#ixzz5Sc4DsxtB. Retrieved from
the internet November 28, 2018 8:11 pm.

Made in the USA
Middletown, DE
14 January 2020

82857769R10116